Ultimate Decorating

Megan Fulweiler

Publications International, Ltd.

Megan Fulweiler is a writer who specializes in home design. She has served for many years as a contributing editor for *Rhode Island Monthly*. Her work—both as a writer and photo stylist—has appeared in a number of publications, including *The New York Times, Traditional Home, Home Magazine,* and *Woman's Day.* Fulweiler is the author of *Relaxing on the Porch* and *Holiday Decorating.*

Louis Weber, CEO
Publications International, Ltd.
7373 North Cicero Avenue
Lincolnwood, Illinois 60712

Manufactured in China.

8 7 6 5 4 3 2 1

ISBN: 0-7853-6010-7

Library of Congress Control Number: 2002109130

Contents

Get Under Way

Every house should be a warm haven, a place where we throw off the cares of the world and relax with family and friends. From the kitchen where we launch our busy days to the bedrooms where we close our eyes at night and dream, we want each space to reflect our personal tastes and sensibilities. But we desire that our rooms be comfortable and practical. Pulling all the components together is a tall order, and yet it's also wonderfully rewarding. Use the bounty of information we've provided here as inspiration, and create the kinds of rooms your loved ones will want to hurry home to enjoy.

Blonde wood, green plants, and an abundance of light instill a dining area with all the airiness of a soft summer morning.
Manufacturer: Thomasville Furniture

Formulate a Plan

On the following pages, you'll find much of the information you'll need to think through every phase of your decorating project from conception to happy completion. Perhaps you want to decorate a brand-new family room, or maybe you're redecorating a vacant bedroom now that a child is grown? Whatever the undertaking, the more attention spent on details, the better the results.

These days, you can choose from scores of materials, finishes, fabrics, and fixtures. Magazines, videos, and books (such as this one) are unending sources for ideas. Neighbors and relatives, especially those who've been down this road before, might have helpful suggestions. And, should you want more guidance, you can turn to a design professional.

A first word of advice: Forging stylish rooms that resonate with character and comfort doesn't happen overnight. Ideally, we would all like to be

This pair of adjoining rooms was revamped with similarly painted walls and ceilings for cohesion. Antique blue plates add zest to inherited furniture.
Designer: Joseph P. Horan, FASID

somewhere else while work is under way, but that's not always possible. Having a sensible plan for how to make do until the workers depart or the paint dries is the next best option. Try not to be tempted to take on the whole house and be done with it. Tackling a single space at a time will better allow you to control the chaos, especially when young children are present. It's easier to empty one room of furniture—and find berths in other rooms for misplaced beds and tables—than three. Overhauling in small increments is also less time- and money-consuming and more immediately gratifying.

On the practical side, when hiring professionals such as carpenters, electricians, and painters, it may be more economical to have them complete all the work within a specific time frame. One lengthy visit will entail more preparation and patience on your part, but savings could be substantial. Be sure to hire a reliable professional who will lay out your options and help you choose the smartest route.

Before the saws buzz and the dust flies, specify one room as your headquarters. A quiet nook where the family can muster for dinner or watch a movie lends stability. If the kitchen is involved, arrange a temporary galley with a fridge near the bathroom. Use the bath sink for water, and be sure to include items you use everyday such as the microwave or coffeemaker. And generate some fun: Colorful paper plates and cups interject a festive picnic air and cut down on cleanup. To safeguard the kids, implement the out-of-sight, out-of-mind concept and devise a separate entrance that segregates the work zone from the rest of the house. Be sure youngsters understand that this area and all its dangerous tools are off-limits.

If you have decided to buy a new house, be sure to work closely with your architect or builder not only in devising blueprints but also as the structure takes shape. If adjustments or substitutions are in the plans, make sure you have final approval. Small changes, such as an extra counter where the kids can hunker down for a snack or no shelf in the bath, will impact how each room functions.

When buying a newly constructed home in a subdivision or development, sign on the dotted line as soon as possible. Purchasing a new home before standard flooring, cabinets, fixtures, and appliances are installed expands your decorating options and eliminates the expense of replacing those materials—the ones you would never have chosen—later. Keep in mind that tract-type builders translate fewer decisions, while semicustom builders generally offer a variety of packages featuring different upgrades along with floor plan options.

If you intend to enlist an interior designer for your new home, involve him or her as soon as possible to help determine color schemes and select appropriate finishes. Your designer should have a copy of the blueprints or just the room, window, and doorway dimensions to choreograph furnishings. Dimensions are also invaluable when it comes to older homes. Ask the seller if they'll allow you to take measurements. You may not be able to fit your queen-size bed through a narrow passageway in a rambling old farmhouse or a cottage. You don't want to learn that on moving day!

Although it's not always feasible, staggering closing times will allow you to work on your new home before you have to vacate the other home. Jobs like painting and repairing are easier when rooms are devoid of furniture and boxes. Even a few days will give you the opportunity to paint the bath and scrub the carpets.

The addition of architectural details like crown moldings and entry columns upgrades the look of this tract home. A subtle mix of patterns and textures also imparts a distinct stylishness.
Designer: Haruko Yoshida, ASID, CID/Integrafika Design Studio

Decorating one room often affects adjoining rooms. If you're content with the space next door, draw on its colors, furnishings, and overall flavor for ideas. Maintaining a similar palette will foster cohesion. If the adjacent room is scheduled for a fix-up at a later date, consider it in your initial plans when picking paint or fabric. If you're hoping to eventually add rooms or remodel other areas of the house, be careful not to put structural elements or plumbing in places that will obstruct future endeavors.

Consider these easy-to-do, unifying tips:

• Blur boundaries by painting rooms the same color, or employ different shades of a similar color with slight tonal variations. You could use pale yellow, golden yellow, and cream in one room. Combine deeply saturated colors (green) with lighter versions (sage).

• Install similar flooring such as sisal, wood, or tile. Floors can also be married by color; for instance, wed light brown tile with a deeper brown carpet. If you're unable to replace the flooring, merge rooms with like-colored area rugs.

• Repeat texture throughout the space. Think velvet drapes in the dining room, velvet-upholstered chairs in the study.

• Employ similar patterns: Dining room chairs with black-and-white-checked fabric could mirror the kitchen's checkerboard floor. Call in different patterns in the same color range, or combine similar patterns in reverse: a raspberry-toned fabric with jolts of white and blue here, blue-toned fabric splashed with raspberry and white there.

• Tie spaces together with architectural elements: wainscoting in the bath and bedroom, chair rails and crown moldings in the living and dining rooms.

Bright murals, along with a decorative ceiling, imbue a small room with cheer. Plentiful storage keeps the space tidy. Use a washable cotton slipcover if you don't want anyone to cry over spilled milk. **Architects: Mojo Stumer Associates**

Every room should reflect your personality and passions, while it also accommodates the way you and your family live, work, and relax. A room that looks heavenly but doesn't live up to your requirements ultimately comes across as disjointed or, worse, unfriendly. For each room, ask yourself the same questions: How do I want this space to appear (cheerful, formal, dramatic)? Who will be using it (adults, children, both)? How should it function (a busy work hub, a niche for relaxation, a place to entertain)?

Do you think you want to use brocade and silk? Don't, if your household consists of children and pets. Washable, long-wearing fabrics are far more sensible. Life is too short to worry over every spill and stain. Put the all-white-living-room theme on hold until the children are grown, and opt for fuss-free upholstery and slipcovers that won't show dog hair. If you crave a more formal tone, achieve it by incorporating deep colors, textures, and patterns. Plan draperies that skim the floor rather than puddle (too tempting for kids and pets). Also, art—paintings, framed prints, or watercolors—will ratchet up the tenor of any room and can be hung high enough so finger and nose smudges won't be issues. Include built-in cabinets or shelves to show off collectibles, but be sure to keep them out of harm's way.

Entertainment units and armoires can serve both adults and kids. Declare the top portion for parents, and designate one or two lower shelves for kids to store their games and storybooks.

Who will be watching television? If more than two people will be, *a* sofa and *a* chair facing the set won't fly. Four or more family members—with visi-

Small children and pets? Not in this elegant room. Luxuriant drapes hitting the polished floor, upholstered dining chairs, and a classic brass chandelier are more appropriate for adult entertaining.

tors coming and going—require a bevy of comfy seats. In addition to a sofa and some chairs, move in oversize floor pillows for lounging. A scaled-down rocker is a welcoming spot for a youngster. And plenty of side tables (make these folding if footage is scarce) fashion a home for snacks and drinks. Because feet seem to like to rest on the coffee table, hunt for one that is solid, and vanquish less-rugged furnishings to another part of the house. Tables with laminate or varnished surfaces will withstand rings left behind by wet glasses.

What about the kitchen, the heart of your home? Do you or any other occupants cook? Do you want to prepare dinner and monitor the kids' homework at the same time? Separate work stations, dual sinks, and properly mapped aisles will foster efficiency, while an island will protect the chef and, at the same time, provide a roost for friends and family.

Equal thought should be carried over to every room. If your bath is frequented by the whole family, it's more important than ever to plan carefully. Along with choosing the proper materials, you'll want plentiful storage for towels and supplies. A pair of sinks, a tub, a separate shower, and a toilet sequestered in its own private compartment will make the space usable for two on busy mornings.

Bedrooms should be sanctuaries. A master suite with a bathroom is the epitome of luxury. But any bedroom rises to new levels of comfort given the proper amenities. Come-rest-awhile furnishings, bedside lighting for reading, a window with a view of treetops and sky? What will please you most?

Of course, sometimes we must plan multipurpose rooms. No dining room? A drop-leaf table set on one side of the living room provides an instant dining area. When company is due, shift the table away from the wall and slide in a bench. Arrange chairs on the opposite side. Think about fashioning a home office with a sofa that opens into a bed to accommodate guests. In order to utilize a small space, select a combination corner table and desk along with hanging shelves. Panache? Have your office chair custom-covered to match the sofa.

Once you've ascertained how a room should function, focus on how you want it to feel and what sort of mood you wish to create. Small gestures such as extra pillows, a soft throw, or a scented candle bring instant ambience. The most effective interiors develop personalities based on lighting, fabrics, furnishings, and color. If you're the perky morning type, zestier colors are for you. Introverts might prefer snugger spaces with less-vibrant hues. Generally (nothing is written in stone), kitchens, family rooms, children's bedrooms, and baths tend to be bright in color. Formal living rooms, dining rooms, and studies lean toward subdued colors and tranquil patterns in limited numbers.

Searching for a special persona, a unique element, or a specific color? Investigate paint and fabric brochures, decorating magazines and books, furniture catalogs, and Web sites of product manufacturers. Look to designer show houses, builder show homes, and your garden. Decorators have long known that the trigger to a whole room can often be something as simple as a summer flower.

In a young girl's room, a romantic sleigh bed, which includes drawers for storage, is both aesthetically pleasing and practical. An inviting window seat also maximizes space. **Designer: Ron Becker, ASID**

The best way to evaluate a room is to empty it. With furnishings, window treatments, and artwork banished, the room's pluses—and minuses—are exposed. Far better to deal with defects at this point than to waste money and effort trying to disguise them later. Check walls, ceilings, windows, and woodwork. Is there glass that needs replacing? Are there plaster cracks?

The basic elements—walls, ceiling, and floor—are central to the overall appearance of your room. Most often, kitchens and baths will show the greatest wear and tear. Sometimes, if you're changing houses, a thorough cleaning of the rooms in the new space instills life. However, these well-used rooms usually require more. Tiles in floors and walls can be regrouted or recaulked. Tubs can be reglazed. Maybe this is an opportunity to upgrade the plumbing. Substituting a standard-size whirlpool tub for a bathtub is a luxurious leap forward. And

A distinctive whirlpool tub has cleverly been given the place of honor. The addition of moldings around the tub and on the wall increases the room's stature. **Manufacturer: Kohler Co.**

small alterations zoom a lackluster bath or kitchen into the limelight, too. Replace the doors on sound but ho-hum cabinets, and bring in new hardware.

Now's the time to find a corner where a closet will fit, add a window, or reconfigure walls and doorways. If you don't want the expense of relocating the toilet, why not compartmentalize it with a half-wall? The wall's top can serve as a shelf for pretty toiletries or plants to increase the sense of privacy. Architectural moldings can transform bare

walls, dull windows, ho-hum cabinets, or an uninteresting fireplace. For that matter, a brand-new fireplace (gas or wood-burning) would give the great room a focal point and the whole house an increased aura of welcome.

Electrical systems often need to be updated, especially in older homes. In addition to more outlets, consider recessed lighting, wall sconces, and ceiling fans. Faced with a blank canvas, you'll begin to see all the possibilities.

Count Your Pennies

Skilled labor and materials add up fast. You don't want your project to become a financial burden. Each step should meet your requirements and reflect your tastes. Rule of thumb? It's best to get structural needs figured out and accounted for first. If you are calling in a contractor, three bids are recommended, and request references. And, if feasible, visit a project the contractor has recently completed.

Trips to home centers, showrooms, and furniture stores will help you establish a realistic figure. If the amount involved isn't large

Simple architecture can be as appealing as high-end construction. A peaked ceiling and wood paneling cozy up this laid-back room—without breaking the bank.

and you'll be able to pay it off in a month or two, the simplest way to handle it may be to put it on a credit card. Remember, though, credit cards often have the highest interest rates. Talk to the employees at your bank, and use the Internet to explore every avenue from home-equity loans to refinancing. Check with the assessor's office, too, to determine the selling prices of homes in your neighborhood. Kitchen and bath upgrades can return as much as 70 to 90 percent of their cost at resale. However, experts caution that it's not wise to invest so much that you significantly raise the value of your home above others in the area. Later, should you decide to sell, it could prove difficult to recoup the money.

If you're handy, lessen expenses by performing a portion of the labor yourself. Discuss this with the contractor, and make sure it's noted in your contract. Ripping up an old floor and hauling away debris are possible money-saving tasks. But use common sense, please: Dangerous materials, such as those involving asbestos or paint containing lead, should be left to the experts.

With all of today's options, high-end materials are not the only answer. Keep an open mind, and when the price is too steep, find a substitute within budget. Can't afford handmade Italian tiles? Ceramic tiles that mimic their warmth and color are an affordable alternative.

Decorators know design is never-ending. You no sooner resolve one room than another challenge arises. As families grow and lifestyles change, rooms evolve. Begin a folder or file containing information pertinent to each room you're currently working on. Store everything from paint chips to fabric samples in your folder. A whopping portion of every project's success is due to careful consideration of all the elements. Include a rough floor plan (with points of access and traffic routes noted), and write down the room's measurements and architectural details. Designate one section for resources like telephone numbers, fax numbers, and Web sites. Set aside a "budget page" so you can tally the money—who's been paid, who hasn't—as the project moves along. Some decorators prefer a standard accordion file with pockets since it allows a pocket for each room; others tout the benefits of a loose-leaf notebook equipped with a durable cover that zips. Keep in mind that pictures, paint chips, and receipts will have to be stapled to the pages of a notebook. However, notebooks are often a bit more advantageous than accordion files, especially when the notebooks have separate pockets to hold scissors and tape measures.

Take inventory of the room's existing furnishings including cabinets, appliances, and accessories. Then, divide that list into three categories: keeps, maybes, and discards. Include dimensions of each piece (height, depth, and width); this will help when you're shopping for a new item or trying to find a home for a discard in another room of your house. Tip: Think about moving questionable furnishings to another part of your home. For example, just because the dresser no longer works in your daughter's room doesn't mean it wouldn't be an appealing addition to the bath. Put the dollars you save by not building a storage cabinet for towels toward a stunning rug for the new space!

The second list you make is your wish list. Include everything you'd like to see in your new room. Try to think of the small activities that take place every day. Would a built-in niche for car keys help keep the room more orderly? How about a spe-

Organizational Skills

Whether you're starting from scratch or redecorating, your new room will look more beautiful and function better if you plan ahead. Divide the elements into three categories: keeps, maybes, and discards. Include the measurements (these will also come in handy if you are looking to substitute new pieces for old) to help devise a manageable and comfortable floor plan as well as a focal point. Once down on paper, you can see what you need as well as the treasures you might already have. If you're envisioning a more formal tone for the dining room, for example, your list might read:

Keeps
Expandable dining table, $59 \times 35 \times 30$ inches high, expands to $90\frac{1}{2}$ inches long
Six dining chairs, $18\frac{1}{2} \times 22 \times 36$ inches high
Wrought-iron chandelier

Maybes
Four framed botanicals, 18×21 inches each

Discards
Flea-market-found, white-painted buffet, $42 \times 18\frac{1}{2} \times 38$ inches high
Cotton café curtains
Floral-patterned wool rug, 9×12 feet

cial spot for the pet's bed? For now, forget costs. If you've always coveted a decoratively painted ceiling swirling with clouds, make a note. Maybe the budget won't stretch to allow for an artist, but hiring a student from a local art school is a possibility. Confronted with a written list, it's easier to determine what you can and can't live without and to find creative solutions.

The more information you assemble, the easier it will be to make known your intentions to a contractor or designer. A picture, it's true, is worth a thousand words. Keep all those magazine photographs handy, and stay organized. When the need arises, you'll be able to open your folder and whip out a picture that illustrates exactly what it is that you want, a measurement, or a carpet sample. It's less stressful on you and the people assisting you if you have samples and swatches to reference, too. Tote your file along when you go shopping or antiquing. When you come across a new light fixture or a lovely old iron bed, you'll be better able to judge whether the find will work or not.

Thanks to meticulous planning, each space in this stunning home complements the other. Choreograph your own harmonious decor by maintaining an up-to-date record of colors and furnishings for every room.

Kitchen and bath upgrades generally require experts and installers who are familiar with building codes, plumbing, and wiring. Structural work demands a licensed architect or designer/builder as well as licensed contractors and skilled tradespeople. Smaller-scale jobs with no construction involved are the safest endeavors for do-it-yourselfers. By doing your own work, you save money, you have control of the schedule, and when it's done *you* get the credit. However, decorating entails time and energy. Be honest with yourself. If you like to sew and hate to paint, make the drapes and hire a painter.

If you're worried about tackling a central-to-family-life room like this spacious kitchen all by yourself, consider recruiting an expert to help with the many decisions.

An interior designer specializes in aesthetics but can also draw floor plans and construction documents. Although not as well trained in dealing with projects that affect the exterior and structure of a house, interior designers who list ASID (American Society of Interior Designers) after their names have received a degree from an accredited school of design, have had full-time work experience, and have passed an exam given by the National Council for Interior Design Qualification. Designers charge for their services any number of ways: Some request a flat fee covering their design and supervision; others charge a retainer for their services and an hourly rate; some add a fixed percentage to designer-discounted prices to yield a profit; and still others use a combination of all these methods. To ascertain which designer is for you, collect references and conduct interviews. Find names by visiting the local chapter of the ASID, trying the Web, or contacting the designers listed in this book's Resource Directory. Equally as important as the designer's portfolio and credentials is how well you bond. You want a designer you feel comfortable with, who understands your goals, and who will do his or her best to see that those goals are met.

Laying the groundwork—determining how the room should function and feel and deciding the best way to finance the job and whether to seek assistance—is a large accomplishment. Now, set aside time to study what good design entails. Once grasped, these basic principles will help you look at every space with a better understanding of what's required to create the perfect setting every time.

Design Basics

Like the recipe for a perfect dish, good design encompasses a number of crucial ingredients. Once you know and understand what these are and why they're needed, you can add your personal stamp—a bit more this, a little less that. You'll be able to visualize and carry out scenarios that measure up aesthetically and practically. A teenager's bedroom? A bookish den? In reality, both should be approached in the same manner. The key elements—scale and balance, color, texture and pattern, and lighting—never change. After acquiring an awareness of the part each plays, you'll feel confident approaching every decorating project.

Cabinetry finished a vibrant shade of blue and apple-red walls are suitable companions for shiny steel appliances. The sculptural range hood offsets the traditional wood floor. **Designer: Jean Kezeor, ASID**

Space and Balance

Reduced to its simplest terms, a balanced room is one that has a visually pleasing arrangement of furnishings, all of which are a comfortable fit or scale for the room. Heights and sizes may and *should* vary for greater vitality, but the juxtaposition is carried out with purpose. For example, to maintain the same visual weight, an armoire should be offset with a generous-size table or two portly chairs, an area rug, and a smaller table. An oversize porcelain bowl displayed on the mantelpiece has two framed watercolors as its neighbors. And keep in mind that no lamp should be bigger than the table upon which it sits.

Lacking the proper mix of scale and balance, a room feels disjointed or even lopsided. Think of a living room where all the furniture is pushed to one side. How much better it would have been to have tugged the sofa away from the wall and anchored it with a table behind and two smaller tables at either end. The end tables don't have to match, but neither one should overpower the other. If you plan to buy new furniture, study the entire room first. Consider what you already own and what you need. Then visualize how the pieces will work with each other. Do as the professionals do: Include some matching elements to add symmetry and to enhance the sense of harmony. Think twin lamps, dual mirrors, two trays, or matching chairs on either side of a hearth for formality.

START DRAWING

A dozen little furnishings afloat in a big—or even a little—room end up looking like clutter as the eye darts from one object to the next. In fact, a few larger-scale pieces can actually make a tiny room appear grander. So they don't

A perfect composition: The weighty, svelte armchair—reminiscent of art deco—and low round table balance the large modern painting. The rug, the art, and the chair share colors, and that contributes harmony.
Designers: Dennis Jenkins & Assoc.

get lost, group small furnishings together in a large room. To avoid having to lug and push, use room-planning aids like computer programs to experiment with a variety of furniture arrangements or draw the room to scale on graph paper. Mark the location of doors and windows, traffic zones, architectural features, electrical outlets, and heating sources. Make one square foot of room space equal to one square. Cut out blocks—to scale again—to represent each piece of large furniture. In a shoe-box-size room, only one option may exist for a tall hutch or an overstuffed love seat. If that's the case, concentrate on finding the most complementary sites for your other furnishings. Consider adding a mirror to enhance the sense of space, and at the same time, begin thinking about creating a focal point.

GRAB THEIR ATTENTION

A focal point is the highlight of the composition; it is the element that draws and holds the most attention. If you're fortunate enough to have a beautiful view from a picture window in your living room, designate the window as your centerpiece, and compose your furnishings to take advantage of it. Fireplaces and French doors are classic focal points. Today a media center tucked discreetly behind louvered doors with matching storage units on either side or a handsome armoire might be an option as well. However, TVs by themselves are not good can-

A handy ottoman organizes a classic arrangement of furnishings using the fireplace as a focal point. Although the shape of the celadon chairs is somewhat different from the shape of the red chairs, their visual weight is balanced.

didates. With the set turned off, TVs are dreary, dark holes.

Sometimes less-obvious focal points gain interest when they are off-center or not placed in the main part of the room. An antique cupboard filled with a collection of your grandmother's majolica, a lovely hand-painted Chinese screen, an oversize painting, or a mass of healthy green plants (lit at night) would each fit this role. You want visitors to stand up and take notice. However, you also need to be aware of practicality. Would two small conversation areas better allow traffic to flow than one? Awkwardly placed tables and chairs that interfere with your

family's movements should be left out. Figure approximately 30 inches for walkways, and position sofas and chairs no more than eight feet apart or people will have to strain to hear one another. In the dining room, three feet of pullout space is required for chairs around a table.

Furniture can also alter the proportions of a room. A sofa set on the diagonal, for instance, widens a space visually. A taller piece such as an armoire makes the ceiling seem higher while also providing a focal point. To foster flexibility in a small room, include one or two movable pieces. When you are seeking extra elbow room for a meeting of the school committee, a streamlined maple coffee table on casters is easy to roll away. If someone in the family uses a wheelchair, make certain there is plenty of room for their maneuverability, and arrange seating so they can conveniently pull up and join in.

In a kitchen where function comes first, layout is paramount. Implement the classic work triangle—the imaginary line that runs from sink to cooking center to refrigerator and back to sink (see page 77 under the *Create a Work Triangle* in the *Puzzle the Pieces Together* chapter)—to save steps and increase efficiency. In the kitchen, the cooking area is often designed as the focal point. A magnificent stone range hood teamed with a backsplash of oversize stone tiles elevates an ordinary drop-in cooktop to dramatic heights. A sculptural stainless-steel hood over a no-nonsense industrial-style range is equally as arresting. Tile gives you leeway to create all sorts of colorful murals and mosaic designs to serve as eye-catchers in both kitchens and baths.

Unleash your imagination! If you own a vintage tub on legs, embellish it with gold and suspend an elaborate chandelier above it. If you're in the process of remodeling and privacy is not an issue, install a large window next to the tub. A generous amount of glass will not only focus attention on the bathing area but will also make the room feel more spalike.

SMALL TOUCHES
TIP THE SCALES

Objects of similar materials—silver bowls at either end of the sofa, silver candlesticks on the mantle—unobtrusively bring harmony to a space. Another option is to use color to unite objects that have no common thread. An inlaid box, a stack of leather-bound books, and a picture frame—each a lustrous shade of burnt umber—will look very content together, not busy, on a glass-topped side table. Don't allow collections to be scattered helter-skelter. Too many things everywhere make a room look cluttered. Muster your treasures on one table or shelf, and the room will appear twice as serene.

Repeat colors within the room, too. Echo the citrus color of a painting in sofa pillows or the luminous green of an Asian lamp in the carpet. Color is one of your best tools.

A shelf as well as a neatly arranged collection of baskets above the cupboard imbues the country furniture piece with greater stature.

Right now, you're probably wearing your favorite hue— taupe, lavender, pink? Studies have shown that color, in every aspect of our lives, affects us emotionally and physically. Orange, for instance, stimulates the appetite. Don't be surprised if you find yourself feeling hungrier in a kitchen or a restaurant that's painted the color of your morning juice. People tend to be more "up" in red rooms, more subdued in those that are blue. Hospital rooms are often painted a pale, serene green, a shade of well-being.

With color you can manipulate the proportions and mood of a room, making it seem smaller or larger, loftier or more intimate. On the whole, rooms washed with an abundance of natural light are best painted either white or a pale color; darker rooms are more attractive in a rich, warm color. No

A striking contrast of red and blue-green provides drama for an equestrian-flavored sitting room. The white trim highlights architectural details and enlivens the two colors. **Manufacturer: Brass Light Gallery**

light in the kitchen? Buttery yellow walls can bring in the sun. Have an upstairs hall that's too long and too narrow? An end wall painted a warm marigold color will dispel that gloomy corridor feeling forever. Tones of sand and blue-gray together are like a day at the shore. Dazzling jewel tones add brilliance. Historical colors such as ochers, reds, and blues (Williams-

burg blue being at the top of the charts) conjure up period backdrops.

All that said, color can often seem the most confusing aspect of decorating. Overwhelmed by hundreds of choices, you have probably forgotten that, unlike lots of other elements you may not be too thrilled with like the tiles on the floor or the shingles on the roof, the wrong color paint is easily remedied. If you don't like it, pick up the brush and try again. Rather than be intimidated by color, use it to forge rooms that make you happy every single day.

WHIRLING THE COLOR WHEEL

You'll feel more confident if you understand how colors interact with each other. The physicist Isaac Newton developed the first color wheel way back in the 17th century when he was studying the effects of a beam of light shining through a prism. The color wheel, consisting of 12 colors, is the prismatic spectrum of rainbow colors set forth as a circle. The three primary colors—red, yellow, and blue—are spaced equally around the wheel. The secondary colors—orange, green, and violet—which are created by mixing two primaries in equal amounts, are set between them. Tertiary colors—colors such as yellow-green, blue-violet, and red-orange—are an equal blend of a primary and a secondary color and make up the

remaining half-dozen colors. All the other colors outside of the wheel are variations of those 12 colors mixed with white or black or each other. When white is added to color, it creates lighter values called "tints." Adding black or gray to a color forms darker tones called "shades." Celery is a very pale tint of green, while avocado is one of its shades. The term "tone" refers to the value, or intensity, of a color.

ARTISTRY

Some of the most successful decorating themes occur when colors of equal intensity or strength are combined; for example, pastels such as pinks and peaches that have a similar lightness or vibrant hues of red, yellow, and blue that share the same depth. If it's zing you want, combine two complementary colors; they're "complementary" because they lie directly opposite each other on the wheel. Red and green, for example, are popular partners often found

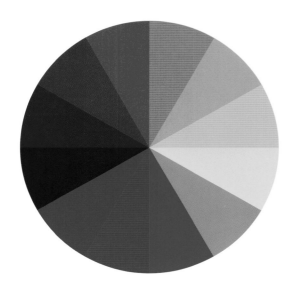

Red stimulates and energizes us, so what better choice for an accent color in a theatrical living room designed for conversation? The vibrant color also helps define the large window.

In the same way a blue sky sets off a summer garden, a blue background enlivens this room but keeps the youthfully slanted space feeling restful. The white trim frames the tableau and animates the blue, pink, and yellow combination. **Manufacturer: 3M Mounting Products with Command Adhesive**

in high-style country rooms. For heightened drama in a stark modern setting of glass and chrome, a less-familiar union would be a purple sofa littered with plump yellow pillows. A color will clash with the colors to the right or left of its complement on the wheel, for instance apricot with purple-blue. Still, not all clashes are bad news. Modernists often pair colors like bright yellow and royal blue successfully.

Cool colors—like green, blue, and violet—will make your living room appear larger because they seem to push the walls away. Warm colors—oranges, reds, yellows—do the reverse. Paint your bedroom a charming Tuscan apricot, and the space will feel marvelously cocoonlike. A dark color will add mystery and romance (on a practical note, dark rooms also remain cleaner-looking longer). A color plan that includes any three consecutive colors or any of their adjacent tints and shades will zap the room with life. Gardeners often follow an analogous scheme in their flower borders with waves of fiery red melting into drifts of orange and yellow or, the opposite, red blooms flowing into crimsons and violets.

Soothing monochromatic themes utilize one color like blue or gray in a variety of tones or gradations. Smoke-colored walls, silvery velvet drapes, and a dark gray sisal carpet on the floor of a New York apartment affords the owner the feeling of living on a cloud. Want to know all your choices for, say, a green scheme? Paint manufacturers have made it foolproof with chips and charts that follow every color's logical progression. To ease our bewilderment, handy aids such as large L-shaped chips exist to judge trim colors and flip charts of suggested color combinations. Some stores even rent pints of a paint for a minimum fee to ease the process along.

Think of your background color as a plate on which you are presenting all the other elements: furnishings, accessories, art. An accent color should be the garnish (the green parsley or the bright red cherry) you place on top. If you appoint a color like cobalt blue or plum as your accent color and adhere to a neutral palette, it will be much easier to shift moods or to alter the look of a room according to season with throws, rugs, cushions, pillows, and slipcovers. A

day's news (think of 1950s pink), an important consideration if you are someday going to place the house on the market.

Kids love color and the more colors the merrier. Kids' artwork is proof. And today there are any number of freewheeling colors based on crayons along with awesome special-effect finishes like glow-in-the-dark paint and glitter. Forego the ubiquitous pale blue and pink for something newer like luscious peach or pale lavender, the color of morning mist. Still, if you're looking to keep the same recipe for a number of years, neutrals such as creamy ivory or pastels will adapt best for them as time goes by and they mature.

Let playful furniture in primary colors be the high jinks for a young child. In an older child's space, one

Splashes of color—the trim around the high windows and the handrails—are just enough to enliven an all-white playroom that relies on light to pep up the children's mood.

pearly colored living room? Come winter, swap lime-green sofa pillows for chocolate-brown. A bright-white-tiled bath? Hang up navy-colored towels as a nautical nod to summer in lieu of red (too winter holidayish). Colors, like fashions, tend to follow the fads. A neutral palette, however, will never look like yester-

color used on all the furniture (white, cornflower blue, or buttercup-yellow) will give the room a tidier, more uniform feel. Rather than installing walls, you could use different colors to designate different areas: Paint the study zone bright green; put restful moss wallpaper behind the bunk beds.

Children appreciate being included in making the decisions regarding their rooms. Rather than confront them with a zillion choices, though, narrow it down to three or four colors you think are appropriate and then let them choose.

Ice-chest white walls and slipcovers keep a seafront home cool and calm during the warmest season. The pale coverings and floor also help blur the boundary between inside and out.

UNBEATABLE WHITE

White or off-white is a timeless background upon which any style can be superimposed. In the 1920s, Syrie Maugham created an all-white drawing room in her London home that became a landmark in the world of interior design. White can be elegant as in an ultramodern loft or homey as in an all-white beach cottage. White unifies a small space. Paint the floor white as well as the walls and windows, and a tiny room will feel more open. Add snowy window treatments—a roll-up shade of white denim, white shutters, or celestiallike white shears—and expand the setting still farther. Contrary to what you might think, white is not boring. Sun-bleached seashells heaped in a bowl offer a host of variations. Follow their cue, and combine several different tones of white: Paint the ceiling a bright, wake-up white; color the walls a more forgiving creamy-white; and dress the chairs and couch in slipcovers of natural cotton. When you need a punch of color, add a bouquet of flowers.

THE FINAL DECISION

Tote home a handful of paint chips or strips in the same color range, and tack them on the wall. Observe how they are affected by continuously changing natural and artificial light. White daylight is made up of all the colors of the spectrum. The color of your walls will depend on how much white light is reflected and how much is absorbed. Switch on a lightbulb that does not have the same balance as the spectrum, and you might notice a more blue or yellow tint.

When you have finally selected your colors or whittled it down to one or two, paint them on a wall and live with them for a couple of days. It will help if you paint a large area rather than just applying a puny dab. If the color seems too dominant, switch to a lighter value on the paint strip. If you're still undecided, trust your instincts. Color is, above all else, very personal. Family and friends aren't going to judge your rooms in technical terms anyway. All they will know is that you're content and that your bedroom looks beautiful. In the end, that's what counts.

Contrasts of smooth and rough, thick and thin, shiny and dull pump up the interest quotient and prevent a room from appearing too staid. That's why the pros mix stripes with checks, pile rugs on tiled floors, and marry leather with wicker. A room full of the same thing is boring. Instead, you could combine surfaces, finishes, and even periods. A 19th-century sideboard, for instance, might hold a pair of stylish lamps from the '30s; in the living room of an urban town house, a raffia armchair could be included to deformalize taffeta drapes. Magic happens when elements with diverse qualities are brought together. Happily, many times, this allows us to use what we have—baskets, books, quilts—in a fresh manner.

Layers—a pillow atop a pillow, chair pads on rush seats, matchstick blinds with cotton drapes—cook up warmth. Especially in cold climates, textures relieve rooms of any sterile or chilly overtones. Of course, how you introduce texture will depend a great deal on the style of your decor and the room's application. An elegant dining room will call for a more subtle hand than a mountain ski retreat. In the dining room, flame-stitch fabric on the dining chairs and a large, heavily textured oil painting is all that's needed. Inside the lodge, Navajo blankets, chenille sofas, and leather armchairs will turn up the heat and form a pleasing interior.

Kitchens and baths exhibit an interesting array of textures. Shimmering surfaces like granite, tile, stainless steel, glass, and mirror are the norm. Even plug-in appliances with their shiny profiles contribute to the picture. But so many hard-edged materials call out for a bit of relief found in a brick hearth, a wood ceiling, or a colorful kilim rug. If you favor a pared-down contemporary style, consider including a warm-hued oak floor or cherry cabinets to mix it up. A butcher-block top on an island, a window seat with a cushion, or a single shelf displaying three or four pieces of rustic pottery in earthlike colors will help balance the overall modernity of the setting.

Be it a flowery needlepoint rug or a stencil used on walls, patterns like textures pick up the tempo of a room and support its theme. Guiding rules? Less pattern in a room that's meant for quiet like a bed-

A handsome hearth is an arresting focal point. Harmony is achieved with a marble-topped table that complements the neutral sofa and a symmetrical arrangement of flowers and seashells on the mantel. **Manufacturer: York Wallcoverings**

room, and exercise restraint when it comes to big, wild patterns. As beguiling as those patterns may seem now, they are the ones you're most apt to tire of quickly. Leopard prints and bold plaid, in the right setting, look fantastic together. However, less-flamboyant rooms will do as well with similar patterns in the same color or with patterns that are not alike but share the same color range. Small-scale repeats in soft furnishings like cushions and upholstery of a larger-scale pattern found at the windows is a well-tested technique. Over the years, certain patterns have become linked with very distinct styles. A faded chintz translates English; a blue-and-white toile is all about France. Study your building blocks—walls, ceiling, and floor—to see how texture and pattern could benefit them.

Ceilings, depending on your decor, can be wall-papered, painted with textured paint, or covered with a material such as tin. Certain heavy papers with embossed patterns can be applied to a ceiling and also painted. Tin ceilings that are most often

In a light-filled kitchen, the use of pattern and color help focus the attention on the breakfast area. The weighty furniture balances the combination of patterns so the result is pleasing instead of overwhelming. **Architect: Clark Robins Design/Build. Inc.; Designer: Douglas B. Leake, CKD; Manufacturer: Style Craft Corp.**

Texture abounds in this elegant bath from the coffered ceiling and handsomely detailed cabinetry to the flowery carpet. Subtle touches—needlepoint pillows, candles, fluffy towels—add more tactile interest. **Manufacturer: Wellborn Cabinet, Inc.**

associated with the 19th century are replicated today in easily installed tiles of steel, brass, or chrome. Tongue-and-groove ceilings, painted or unpainted, are traditional in New England's seaside houses and also on porches.

If you're building a new house, keeping the beams exposed in, say, the family room will add country-house charm as well as texture. Suspend baskets, bunches of dried herbs or wildflowers, or strings of heady garlic from the beams, and gain yet another tactile bit of interest. A ceiling draped with fabric or tented is romantic or fun. Bold red-and-white stripes, for instance, imbue a child's room with a jolly circus ambience. Fabric is an age-old wall treatment, too—from vibrant wall hangings to voluminous curtains suspended from rods affixed just below the ceiling. Quality fabrics such as ticking, wool, burlap, or imitation suede can also be glued to walls like paper. Rather than dress the whole room, consider covering one wall behind a four-poster bed or a writing desk. Upholstered walls also add texture and, with batting underneath, are a high-end remedy for battling obtrusive noise.

Decorative paint treatments such as dragging or sponging are relatively easy and will also hide wall imperfections. And realistic, nature-inspired wallpapers interject texture, pattern, and style. Consider ones like grass cloth or cork for an Asian- or Caribbean-inspired room, or choose papers that simulate bamboo, stone, or wood. Some papers also copycat faux finishes, murals, and architectural details such as plaster ornamentation and wood moldings. To help you achieve a custom look, many of the sample wallpaper

This quiet scene pulses with excitement due to its textural ingredients. A silvery lamp, a black table, and green plant near a rough-as-a-garden-path mirror equal sheer energy. **Designer: Darryl Wilson Design**

books are set up to display complementary colors, patterns, and textures all together. Transport several sample books home, see how the papers are affected by light, and observe which ones will best suit your furnishings before you order.

Even at ground level, texture and pattern matter. Luckily, scores of choices exist for all kinds of spaces and styles. Choose your material according to how the room is used as well as how you want it to look. In a kitchen, the options could be anything from resilient rubber flooring like you might find in busy restaurants to rustic terra-cotta tiles like you might find in Mediterranean homes. Cement with wood inlays is a good-looking partner for commercial-style appliances in a contemporary or a country kitchen.

Play a little! If the room is carpeted, layer on some area rugs to bring it up to date. For a quick breath of summer, toss a sisal rug down on a hardwood floor, and lay a colorful floor cloth out in the sunporch. Even in a tiny powder room, a small easy-to-launder throw rug (anchor it on a no-skid mat for safety) reverberates with style.

Pattern steals the show in this retro kitchen. The vintage stove can't hold a candle to the graphically designed island that looks lively enough to get up and dance.

Lighting

Nothing kills a romantic dinner faster than glaring lights. The soft flicker of a candle or a lantern plays to our moods, giving the scene just the right amount of intriguing glow. At the reverse end of the scale, a home office requires a good deal of light for reading documents and writing. With these examples in mind, consider the mood and the function of the room you are creating. A bedroom may need only assorted table lamps to feel and function properly, while a kitchen demands a full menu from task lighting for performing specific chores safely to overall ambient light to render the room friendly.

Of course, natural light is the most welcoming light of all. Rooms with a surplus of windows or a bank of French doors tend to be more cheerful. A large skylight positioned over the breakfast table or in the bedroom allows the sun to pour in, and with it, up go our spirits. A glass-block window in a shower or beside a bathtub floods the bathing area with sunshine but protects our privacy so we gain the best of both worlds. Look around. Perhaps you can squeeze a window in on the stair landing, in the bathroom, or in the laundry room, transforming what was a dingy throwaway area into a bright space.

Employing the benefits of both natural and artificial light is a good way to reach a happy medium. Lighting specialists plan light in very technical terms using site-specific math-

A lofty room demands a lighting fixture with presence. A masterly chandelier—outfitted with a flock of fabric shades—holds its own. More sedate wall sconces provide additional illumination. **Architect: Latina Homes; Manufacturer: Kichler Lighting**

Shade-Savvy

Sometimes just a new shade—trimmed with beads or fashioned of a playful animal print—will catapult a lamp into the future. Instead of trying to find a ready-made shade that matches a particular wallpaper or fabric, it will be easier if you custom-order one or allow the shade to provide an accent color. Custom-ordered shades (a lamp store can refer you to a source) are more expensive but well worth the cost. An expert will craft a shade out of anything you desire from silk to handmade paper.

To procure the proper fit, take your lamp along with you with the bulb you're planning to use in place. Before you finalize the sale, ask the salesperson to turn on the light. Light changes the appearance of a shade. And here's another secret: Pristine white shades, despite their innocent look, will sometimes make a room appear dingy. Consider a high-energy color instead.

A lamp's bulb and harp (the two-piece element used to secure the frame) should remain hidden from sight. And, in general, the shade should not be taller than the base. If you unearth the right shade but it sits too low, buy a shade riser. A shade riser is a postlike adapter, available in varying sizes from $1/2$ inch to 2 inches, that screws into the top of the harp to lift the shade so it sits higher on the base.

It might seem like endless variations are available when it comes to lamp shades. Avoid confusion by keeping the six basic styles in mind. And feel free to experiment as well. A little serendipity is good.

- *Square- and rectangle-shaped shades complement square or almost square bases.*
- *Drum shapes team best with column lamps.*
- *Ovals are often preferred in tight spaces since they can be pushed against a wall.*
- *Bell shapes, seen frequently in Asian-style rooms, partner happily with urn- or vase-type bases.*
- *Empire shades—narrower at the top than the bottom—mesh well with all sorts of bases.*
- *Coolie shades have an outdated name, but their classic, wide, hatlike shape continues to be a favorite atop a wide base.*

ematical equations to achieve their results. If you're remodeling, don't miss the opportunity to make some fundamental improvements. A pro's expertise can transform the interior and exterior of your home. Cognizant that the correct amount of light enhances the way we live, specialists remember even the small details such as low-voltage lights in closets and spotlights to show off your paintings. Whatever your plan—remodeling or upgrading the lighting you already have—it will help to get an overall sense of what kinds of lighting are available and how each performs before you shop. Lighting stores have designers on hand to answer questions and to help you make the best choices. Although no rules govern how much light a specific room warrants, a number of guidelines exist.

Turn It On

Figure every room needs an average of 200 watts for every 50 square feet. Bulbs with higher lumens (an international unit that refers to the amount of light a bulb produces) are more efficient given the same wattage (the amount of electrical current consumed by the bulb). Packages list both lumens and wattage so it's easy to check. Elderly family members may require more wattage to be comfortable. Your eyes' pupils, as you age, have less flexibility and demand

Subtle lighting showcases the home's Southwestern-spiced architecture, the juxtaposition of materials such as glass and stone, and the owner's collectibles.
Architect: Ron Robinette; Builder: Old Pueblo Remodelers; Designer: Lori Carroll, ASID, IIDA

the wattage of the bulbs. Keep in mind that where the light source is located, what the colors of the walls and furnishings are, and what kind of a shade the light wears will make a difference.

Lightbulbs vary, too. The most common—incandescent bulbs—have a tungsten filament and produce a yellowish white light. Fluorescent bulbs use just a fraction of the electricity that incandescent bulbs do and last up to 20 times longer; this is the reason they are so often used in commercial settings. We usually think of fluorescent bulbs as slim tubes, but they can also be purchased as screw-in types to be used in place of incandescent bulbs in a standard light socket. Look for them in a rainbow of quirky, fun colors or, to impart a more natural cast, warm white. Halogen bulbs emit an extremely bright, white light,

greater brightness. Studies show an average 50-year-old gets as much light from a 100-watt bulb as a 20-year-old gets from a 50-watt bulb!

When you want to increase lighting in, say, the family room, either double the amount of light sources or, if the fixtures can take it (be sure wattage never exceeds a manufacturer's recommendation), double

which makes them useful as spots and downlights. These also have a longer life and provide more lumens per watt than regular incandescent bulbs. On the downside, halogen lights, which closely mimic daylight, generate intense heat and can pose a greater fire hazard. A halogen light should never be put near a curtain or come in contact with plastic materials.

A proper lighting plan will include the right combination of ambient (overall) lighting to illuminate the space, task lighting to provide illumination for specific activities such as reading or playing games, mood lighting to create an agreeable atmosphere, and accent lighting to focus attention on specific objects like that new sculpture in the living room. Install dimmers on your lighting fixtures in order to fine-tune—increasing or decreasing—the illumination as you choose.

Lighting Fixtures

There's no set rule that dictates you must have a traditional fixture in a traditional room just as there is no real reason that lamps—safely installed—need to be quarantined to the usual spots. Try one on top of the vanity or on the kitchen counter. An unexpected element like an ornate chandelier over a country table or a hanging pendant lamp with a pale silk shade by a chintz-covered chaise just increases the dynamics. Matching the style of the room to the style of the fixture, though, will help focus and narrow your search. An electrician's labor is fairly expensive so it's backward economy to buy anything less than the best quality and most wanted fixtures you can afford.

Generally, contemporary fixtures in materials such as polished chrome and stainless steel are at home in ultramodern settings; traditional fixtures like candlesticks, porcelain ginger-jar lamps with cloth shades, sconces, wrought-iron standing lamps, and banker's lamps—just to name a few—are most content in traditional settings. Track lights, with halogen or incandescent bulbs, are perfect for any situation—kitchen, family room, or office—because you can aim the light exactly where you want it.

And, more costly since they involve construction, recessed spotlights or floodlights will provide any room with ambient or task lighting. A favorite of decorators, unobtrusive recessed lights fit every room style. Make a lighting list, and carry it with you when you start out. Remember a great-looking fixture derives as much attention as an art object. If you find one you know is perfect for your decoration, don't pass it by!

Room by Room

For the bedroom, versatile and popular swing-arm lamps, available in any number of finishes and looks, render nighttime reading enjoyable and leave bedside tables free for books and other paraphernalia. Include a three-way switch for a choice of light level, and position the lamp no more than 12 inches away from the bed. Swing-arm lamps will work anywhere space is constricted such as near a desk or phone. Overhead fixtures should be selected to echo the room's style. Forego a mundane institutionallike fixture for a reproduction-period light, a modern hanging lamp in glass and steel, or a zany ceiling spotlight with a trio of adjustable halogen lights. Standing floor lamps used to be quite routine but no longer. How about a torchère with a lacquered steel base and a plastic, sherbet-colored shade to jazz up your teenage daughter's room?

According to style, a living room can easily be enhanced with recessed lighting or the appropriate sort of overhead fixture such as a low-voltage chandelier or a pendant lamp used primarily for decorative purposes. At a minimum, a small living room should also include four table lamps or a combination of floor and table lamps to form plenty of welcoming pools of helpful illumination. Tiny low-voltage halogen uplights (inexpensive can lights that sit on the floor) throw light up to be reflected from walls and ceilings. Also inexpensive and portable, popular uplights are a fine way to provide indirect light when recessed lighting is out of the question.

Family rooms and dens—home to all sorts of activities—demand general background illumination just as living rooms do. Table lamps and downlights will provide ample light whether family members are reading or playing a game of chess. As a rule, the bottom edge of the lamp shade should be at eye level of the person seated near it. If you want a standing lamp to function for reading, stand it behind the chair. For safety, run exposed cords along the baseboard or behind furniture—never under a rug. You don't want the light from a fire to be a source of illumination.

A chandelier suspended over a dining room table (about 30 inches above is the norm) acts as a focal point while shedding light on delicious meals, welcome guests, and other objects that tend to gather there. To foster a stay-and-linger sort of mood, though, it's wise to include a dimmer. When you need the table for another job like laying out a sewing pattern or going over bills, it will be easy to pump up the brightness. For a low level of general illumination in the dining room, sconces and low-voltage recessed lights are often included along with a chandelier.

Kitchens require light in every square foot. A good-quality ceiling fixture or recessed or track lighting will prove invaluable.

In a far greater way than other lamps, chandeliers—in this case, a handsome pendant—contribute to the style of a room as well as shed some light. **Manufacturer: Brass Light Gallery**

Note that the wattage will need to vary according to the color of your walls and surface treatments as well as their reflecting values. A forest-green counter, for example, will absorb light and may make food preparation dangerous. Be aware that adequate lighting sources should be installed directly above the range and the sink, the situations where you least want shadows for preparing and cooking. Strip lights mounted beneath the cabinets will illuminate work spaces below—so you'll at least see your finger before you accidentally cut it.

Bathrooms—where we primp and groom—need high-voltage lighting especially near the mirror. If you want, hunt for fixtures that duplicate the era of an older room or create some romance there instead: Sparkly crystal sconces near an etched mirror over a delicately skirted sink would be especially pretty. Bracketed fixtures or sconces could be situated on either side of a mirror or medicine cabinet, or a light could be positioned right above the mirror. A waterproof fixture in the shower is always helpful and necessary. The specific level of light necessary will depend on the room and your personal preferences. For instance, you might want to include a dimmer so you can soften the mood while you enjoy a long, leisurely herbal soak.

An Arts and Crafts-style fixture illuminates the grooming area while maintaining the character of an older home. **Manufacturer: Brass Light Gallery**

Now that you have a sound idea of the kind of elements you'll want to consider, the next step is finding your style. If you're drawn to clean lines and subdued colors, you may feel more at home in a contemporary setting. Flowery patterns and sweet colors sound good? Then, a English-country or traditional bedroom may be for you. Finding your way to the perfect look will lead to a new, lifelong form of self-expression.

Traditional needn't be boring. A striking dog portrait, luxurious fabrics, and a careful measure of accessories give this creamy-colored living room lasting appeal.
Designer: David M. Plante

Every style includes distinguishing elements: brass candlesticks and highboys, for instance, translate Colonial; curvaceous side chairs and wall-hung porcelain dishes speak to French provincial. If you're searching for a style, compile a list of favorite rooms. Maybe you like your grandmother's kitchen or a friend's library? What can you borrow from those rooms to forge your own perfect space? Finding a style that suits your lifestyle and setting doesn't mean starting over so don't panic. Furnishings are recyclable; heirlooms blend. The rigid rules of the past are gone. Have the style you want your way. Familiarizing yourself with popular modes of decoration will jump-start those creative juices.

Tasteful Traditional

In the strictest sense, a traditional room is one that adheres to a certain period of history such as Georgian or neoclassical. In general terms, however, traditional style has come to translate a generous mix of highly polished pieces from any number of periods and countries (or good quality reproductions) and luxurious accoutrements. Cary Grant and Grace Kelly would look as if they were at home in a traditional-style living room. Today, however, thanks to a newer, fresher take, so would many young families.

Older homes frequently have decorative trim and detailing that partner perfectly with such a refined decor. In a newer house, adding architectural embellishments and applying decorative paint techniques (stippling and combing are two examples) will help foster background elegance. Thick Oriental rugs resting on gleaming hardwood floors, skirted tables, and gilt-framed mirrors are typical in traditional rooms. So are elaborate window treatments such as tassel-trimmed swags and jabots.

A fresher modern approach, however, shifts these classic-looking rooms to a lighter palette. As opposed to rich warm tones like red and yellow, walls are washed in taupe, cream, or pale lavender. Window dressings become tailored drapes, sheers, or shades. Still, no matter if the tone is sophisticated or more relaxed, the emphasis is on comfort. A traditional living room decorated with furniture in classic shapes and styles—despite how formal it may look—is always an invitation to make yourself at home. For instance, if an inherited Empire sofa is included, the seat cushions have been revamped for pleasant sitting. Think curl-up-and-finish-that-novel wing chairs and camelback sofas.

To foster conversation, furniture is usually arranged with great symmetry in companionable groupings. Guests never have to hunt for a place to set down a drink or a magazine because every sofa and chair has a table at its disposal. Depending on the tone of the room, upholstery is simply handled or lavish with decorative trimming. Fabrics vary widely: brocade and cut velvet in a stately 19th-century home; linen or wool when the approach is pared-down.

Lighting, an important part of the equation, is carefully manipulated with a combination of table and standing lamps

Adam-style shield-back chairs and a Duncan Phyfe table summon family and friends for many a holiday dinner. Metallic-painted wallpaper on the walls and ceiling adds to the traditional charm. **Designer: Sandra Elizabeth Clinger**

A traditional bedroom with heavy Victorian overtones is rendered more romantic with filmy lace curtains and a vintage crocheted bedspread and tablecloth.

enhance the way the room is used: a bench at the end of a four-poster bed, a set of armchairs, and a writing desk. For a traditional viewpoint in the bath? A tub paneled in classical moldings, luscious materials like white marble for the floor and walls, or a black-and-white-tiled floor and painted walls. Mahogany or lustrous cherry, furniturelike cabinetry (or an antique buffet or chest converted to serve as a vanity) also helps cast the right spell.

Similar furniturelike cabinetry and highly polished granite countertops can sweep the look through to the kitchen, too. Include a number of glass fronts for displaying pretty china and silver; select appliances and hardware (polished brass is a winner) that blend rather than stand out; and install a warm-colored wood or brick floor as a unifying element. The grand finale? A lavish balloon shade at the window to balance a magnificent range hood or, in step with a relaxed sensibility, a pair of unpainted wood shutters the color of a handsome leather-bound book.

GET THE LOOK

- Add bookshelves—the more, the better—and fill them with books.
- Embellish upholstered chairs and sofas with decorative welting.
- Create vertical drama: Install oversize mirrors; mount curtains up high.
- Mix silk with sisal, porcelain with pottery, or wood with silver for contrast.
- Remove rugs, and allow polished floors to shine.

to provide adequate illumination for large gatherings or a party of one who is reading by the fire. Oil paintings, sporting prints, and assorted objets d'art are de rigueur in timeless traditional rooms. In fact, carefully controlled clutter—piles of art books, plaster busts, an old globe—are important elements of the welcoming ambience. Contemporary accent pieces, fabrics and art can also figure in, but nothing is too glaringly new. A lean-cuisine traditional room would edit out the extras, keep the furnishings minimal, and let the architecture shine through.

In the bedroom? Family photographs, ultrafeminine dressing tables, and furnishings that

Convivial Country

The search for country things—painted and unpainted furniture, quilts, baskets, folk art—began in the '20s and '30s when a few savvy collectors realized their merit. By the late '70s, there was a full-blown craze for ladder-back chairs and spongeware. All of America had been introduced to the enduring beauty of handmade rag rugs and quilts. It was the beginning of a welcome, livable approach to decorating, and it helped fan a new enthusiasm for antique-hunting, flea markets, and tag sales that is still evident today. Well-known decorators like Sister Parrish had incorporated country pieces into their designs for years, but now everyone was on the bandwagon. Versatile treasures like tilt-top tables and Windsor chairs were suddenly in vogue in upscale Manhattan apartments.

In the years that have passed, country elements have grown no less popular. A more sophisticated and refined approach now exists, but the appreciation for handmade, well-crafted furniture and accessories has continued and broadened with each generation. Visited over the years by countless influences and assimilating design contributions from around the world, "country" has evolved into an umbrella term encompassing American, English, and French styles as well as those detailed below. Even rustic Adirondack chairs, the colorful Native American blankets and rugs of the Southwest, garden furniture from across the Atlantic, and early 19th-century porcelain china have found a place in country style. Components differ according to a variety of factors like personal taste and region, but every country room, whether trimmed down in a more contemporary mode or rich with layers lovingly collected over time, exudes a comfortable, relaxed spirit and so can yours.

APPLE-PIE AMERICAN

The simple, unpretentious look of American country is easily adaptable. Create warm, cozy

Contemporary furnishings are an interesting foil for an antique stove. The marriage of old and new, along with a light palette, gives the room an up-to-date country mood.

rooms as the early settlers did, or like a flag unfurling, aim for open, more modern country spaces. What can be the starting point? Colors like our Founders knew—cheery barn-red, yellow, dark green, gray, buttermilk, rust, and straw—or marriages of neutral walls with trim done up in heady colors such as blue and wine-red. For a contemporary country look, especially in a small space, paint your room's walls, trim, and ceiling cream or soft white.

Floors? Refinish wood floors to reflect light and show off their grain, or paint a classic pattern of diamonds as a stunning foil for a carefully composed vignette of classic 18th- and 19th-century American antiques. Prefinished look-alike wood floors—available in a variety of wood types—are an up-to-date alternative for heavily trafficked rooms like kitchens and living rooms. Floorcloths, flat-weave rugs, and thick rag rugs help pump up the interest level.

Let the breezes tug at the hems of simple window treatments. Roman shades or half curtains in natural fabrics like cotton, linen, and wool are alluring. From seat cushions to table napkins, you will find simple, off-the-loom patterns work best. For instance, look to plaids, checks, and stripes, in hues like spongeware-blue, lime-green, and butter-yellow.

Furnishings are restrained but welcoming for friends and family. Sofas and chairs should be constructed for years of sitting; dining tables should be generous enough for a crowd; beds should be indulgent: piled with blankets and pillows in winter, stripped down to fresh-off-the-line cotton sheets in summer. Choose accessories to foster an American country attitude: patchwork quilts to hang as art, baskets, hand-carved toys, tinware, and chunky creamware pitchers and bowls. Clean-lined Shaker or raised panel cabinets, a mix of glass and solid doors together, or a combination of wood-tone and painted cupboards will keep the momentum going in the kitchen. Show off your collection of black iron pans or copper pots without letting them jumble; a few favorites are best. As for the bath, claw-foot tubs and old-style sinks are readily available today. Or a standard white tub encased in tongue-and-groove paneling or slate is another idea our ancestors would applaud. Lay durable ceramic tiles in countrylike checkerboard designs on walls and floors; include Shaker-style peg rails to hold towels and robes; and designate wooden cabinet hideaways for everyday toiletries. As night falls, light the candles in a wrought-iron chandelier. American country style is a celebration of simplicity.

GET THE LOOK
- Recruit reproduction Windsor chairs to paint in new country colors.
- Hunt for old burnished wood pieces to lend authenticity.
- Anchor small items on trays or in baskets.

OOOH LA LA

How could French country—also known as French provincial—be anything less than charming? France is renowned for its food, its wine, and its appreciation of the good life and all things romantic including its well-loved 18th-century toile de Jouy (commonly referred to as just "toile") patterns peppered with endearing images of pastoral life. Today, in a rainbow of colors as well as hip black and white, toile is available as everything from wallpaper to accessories. Build a living room around a striking black-and-white combination or a bedroom featuring a soft blue toile the color of a wildflower. Because toile generally has only one color on a neutral background, it mixes pleasingly with patterns. Layer in striped, checked, or solid accent pillows that use the dominant color from your print. Typical French-country window treatments include lace, cotton, or simple panels of unbleached linen hung from iron rods; in a more formal country room, try striped taffeta in a sunbaked shade like tangerine! White or color-washed walls in soft tones like peach, honey, and dusty rose combined with a terra-cotta-tiled floor are guaranteed to evoke a French mystique.

For furnishings, look to gently curved armchairs, a decoratively carved or painted armoire (the most important furniture piece in provincial homes, armoires can be traced back to the 14th century and can serve today's needs by housing your TV), a farmhouse dining table, and simple ladder-back chairs with rush seats. If you have trouble finding antique versions of all your wanted French decor, furniture manufacturers offer a wealth of fitting reproductions including beguiling sofas and love seats to combine with antiques and tag-sale finds.

To imbue a kitchen or bath with the flavor of Provence, choose cabinetry with an antique white or mellow wood finish. And suspend a chandelier with dainty fabric shades from the ceiling. Consider adding French elements such as paintings or prints echoing the impressionist's palette, hand-painted tiles, murals, glazed or unglazed pottery, and delicate bed linens to complement a carved pine or fruitwood bed.

GET THE LOOK
- Include one or two more formal pieces along with casual furnishings.
- Re-cover the seats of curvy armchairs with cheerful checks or stripes.
- Hang a collection of pretty porcelain plates on the wall instead of a painting.

With dog paintings, a hutch filled with decorative dishware, and a come-gather scrubbed pine table, this English country dining room is as inviting as a spot of tea.

- Incorporate more curves, such as a wire lamp or plant stand, a still-life of finials along the mantel, or a half-round table with cabriole legs.

TEA FOR TWO

English country is confident; patterns, colors, furniture styles, and periods are mixed. Nix anything that appears too new; time's patina is perfect. Sun-bleached chintzes in all the colors of a summer garden and slightly worn rugs—piled atop a sea of sisal or a bare wood floor—mimic a Cotswold farmhouse.

Evoke a British mood by painting walls the color of thick cream to maximize light. For richness, introduce jolts of ocher (deep reddish brown) or cantaloupe. Wood paneling up to dado (the lower part of the wall) level is very pretty. Paint or wallpaper the upper portion of the wall with thin stripes, a small geometric design, trellises, or flowers. Create a subtle link between the wallpaper and the slipcovers with color or pattern but nothing too studied; the most charming English country rooms look as though they have slowly evolved. Tartans, tweeds, paisley shawls, chenille, cashmere, or simple gingham, the choice of fabrics allows something for almost every taste. Window treatments can be straightforward, unlined curtains or, for a more formal hardwood cabinets would cheerfully complement freestanding pieces like cupboards and hutches.

GET THE LOOK
- Pluck your color scheme from a collection of English chintzware porcelains you've amassed on a shelf.
- Designate a tray-style table as a coffee table.
- Order roomy slipcovers for comfy down-filled seating.
- Replace the inset of a kitchen door or dining room cabinet with shirred gingham.

A FARMHOUSE IN THE HILLS

Tuscan country is a seductive mosaic of pattern, texture, and color. More tactile than any of the other styles, the Tuscan or Mediterranean demeanor features rough-plastered walls in sun-washed hues and hard floors of terra-cotta tiles, stone, cement, or unpolished marble. It's a look that favors warm climates, but due to modern technology, it's possible even in northern regions where ambient heat can render floors as warm as toast. And, these days, paints of many colors are available to replicate the effects of sun and age.

Furnishings and accessories are carefully chosen and kept to a minimum in Mediterranean homes. A dining room, for example, may hold only an antique table and a handful of carefully edited, mismatched chairs. Offsetting the minimalist arrangement could be opulent window treatments (velvet drapes with sheers, for instance) or a tapestry wall hanging reminiscent of an ancient mural. Cook up your own Roman spell with pictorial wallcoverings depicting rural scenes. Unpainted furniture, pottery, baskets, and candle-holding sconces give more flavor to the Tuscan home.

Country's Mediterranean side shines through in this stone-floored room. A coy mix of white and dark wicker along with a sprightly dash of iron and tile? Ah, Tuscany!

country-estate scene, a valance pared with drapery panels.

What furnishings do you need to complete the English country look? Consider timeless varieties such as comfy sofas and armchairs in the living room, a chaise by the bedroom window, or a scrubbed pine dining table. Coordinate heirlooms with flea-market finds, and arrange informal displays of collectibles. In the kitchen, fine-grained

- Stage a utilitarian centerpiece; for instance, fill a large iron basket with fresh fruit on a tile counter.
- Order a deep soapstone sink.
- Lay a tapestry runner down the length of a rustic table.

RUSTIC BRAVADO

Similar to American style but more eclectic, rustic country includes exposed roughhewn wood beams, open rafters, and wide-plank floors. It's a pioneer cabin kind of ambience that calls for a fire on the hearth, a supply of cozy textiles, and a warm palette of earth tones accented with autumnal hues like red and gold. Many of the treasures you would find in a lakeside camp or mountain hideaway are here: a freshwater pike mounted over the fireplace, a pair of snowshoes in the corner, a fishing rod by the door. Vintage signs and old photographs adorn the unpainted, wood-paneled walls. In addition to twig rockers and settees, there are comfy sofas and chairs slipcovered in plaids or large, cotton checks. Windows are bare or fitted with simple burlap panels or wood shutters. Accessories? Look to hand-blown bottles, pressed ferns under glass, birdhouses, and, the topper, a real canoe hoisted to the ceiling!

Inspired by Southwestern decorating, forgo paneling for stucco or plaster walls, and stockpile colorful Native American blankets and rugs. A terracotta floor and a few pieces of ebony wrought iron nod to the region's colonial Spanish influence; a bleached cow skull is a tribute to Southwest painter Georgia O'Keefe.

A ski lodge could take it up a notch, substituting leather-upholstered seating and faux-fur throws (to toss on chairs and beds) for hooked rugs and

afghans. If the structure permits, make everything from your four-poster bed to the potted cactus in the dining room overscaled to dish up home-on-the-range, big-sky magic.

GET THE LOOK

- Collect vintage Pendleton and Beacon blankets to display on sofas and over chairs.
- Lay folksy patterned rugs beside beds and in front of sinks.
- House electronic gear in a distressed cabinet or an antique pie safe with tin-paneled doors.

Country style with a Southwestern twist: exposed beams, stucco walls, and a massive hearth. Prominent stitching on the chair, footstool, and lamp shade are also in keeping with the rugged ambience.
Designer: J. Mike Patrick;
Manufacturer: New West

Cool Contemporary

Contemporary style embraces unclut- tered, light-filled spaces, open floor plans, minimal furnishings, and slick finishes. Within those perimeters, though, different avenues can be pursued. One approach is dramatic in a subtle manner; the other is a stand-up-and-take-notice kind of deco- rating, saturated in vibrant color. Which route is for you?

Unlike the old days when modern meant stark, laundry-white walls, today's monochromatic rooms are done up in soothing shades like sand, gray, or cream. A burgeoning interest in the environ- ment has designers also culling tones from the outdoors such as pale green and blue to offset light wood and metal fur- nishings. Gone is the outdated marriage of black and chrome that was hot in the '80s. Materials such as metal, glass, and stone are brought together instead, in numerous innovative ways.

Furnishings are likely to include clean-lined chairs and tables in intrigu- ing shapes and forms as alternatives to antiques. Upholstery is impeccably tailored, and slipcovers often include pert dressmaker details like a row of dainty buttons or a demure bow. No jarring patterns, no ubiquitous accents of red. If there are window treatments, they are slimmed down and designed to blend rather than contrast with the wall color. Choices include fabrics that drape well like silk, rayon blends, and wool; or shades and blinds of alu- minum, vinyl, or split bamboo. No flounces, no

Clean as a whistle, no clutter in sight! This stylish room has banished pattern and color to enhance its small size and to maintain a slick, modern profile. **Architect: Angelo Luigi Tartaglia**

frills. In sophisticated bare-bone settings such as these, artisanship is what counts.

The proper accessories add to the look but avoid the bric-a-brac buildup. Clean, uncluttered surfaces enhance a contemporary space. What would suit the occasion? A collection of silver desk objects from the '30s and '40s displayed on a glass-topped table, a pair of salvaged finials on the mantel, or a group- ing of dusky but pretty pottery (also from the '30s and '40s) lined up smartly like soldiers in a built-in bookcase. Pairs of lamps, urns, and vases will provide harmony.

Along the other popular contemporary road: Bold color sings through rooms, defines living areas, and helps to create detailing, which is often lacking in a new design. Ranch houses respond better than older houses to this sort of razzle-dazzle treatment, but color will enliven all sorts of spaces and forge gallerylike scenes to help enrich vivid paintings, prints, and posters. Combine mid-20th-century modern furniture with new designs like skinny upholstered chairs and leather-covered seats with built-in shelving. To prevent a buildup of kinetic energy, large upholstered pieces such as sofas are best done in neutral fabrics. A careful arrangement of shapes and forms—round, square, or rectangular—will interject more interest than a hodgepodge of patterns. If you want to make a statement, a custom-designed area rug that echoes the room's colors can be the icing on the cake.

Architect-designed fixtures, high-tech elements, and luscious materials create a contemporary aura for kitchens and baths, be they of the quiet and serene school or lively color camp. But just changing surface materials can catapult a room into the present. Stainless steel, tile, laminates? Research all the possibilities. If you're remodeling the kitchen, consider a layout that allows for a sleek, functional island in a modern shape; choose no-nonsense industrial-style appliances; and consider the pros and cons of in-vogue (but also long-lasting) materials like cement that can be tinted in appealing earth tones for counters and floors. Select lighting fixtures and hardware carefully as they'll play a more prominent role in rooms that are devoid of clutter. Everything in a contemporary setting from audio gear to grooming supplies should have its place, which—on the flip side—means less cleaning and daily tidying up for you.

GET THE LOOK
- Conceive an aura of calm with all-natural materials like leather, suede, and cement.
- Hunt for affordable reproductions of classic furniture designs displaying geometric forms.
- Minimize accessories.

No matter if you are a chef or a business executive, you will feel connected in this cool kitchen where usable space translates counters for cooking and office work. Part entertainment center, the room hosts a television as well as all the electronics necessary to conduct business. **Architect: William C. Petrone/Sidnam Petrone Gartner Architects**

Excellent Eclectic

An eclectic room is more telling of its creator than other kinds of decor. Compiling diverse furnishings, fabrics, finishes, and objects from any number of periods and countries, it's possible to arrange a totally unique scene. Not bound by any rules, you're free to include whatever you like. Of course, in order to be successful, you'll want to keep all the principles concerning form, scale, composition, and proportion in mind. But, the more original, the better. The only requisite is comfort. You and your family and friends will never appreciate a space if it doesn't provide basics like agreeable seating and good lighting.

Not surprisingly, bedrooms tend to be naturally eclectic. Along with one or two favorite pieces—the bed, say, and a chest you've had since childhood—odds and ends accumulate, such as a rocker that won't do in the living room or an old portrait. The result can be charming, but it's not guaranteed. Beware, decorators warn, of a messy overload. In a living room or a great room, eliminating wallpaper and decorative finishes for a neutral palette is the safest route. Various styles mix congenially when the background and furniture forms are simple. If whites and creams leave you cold, choose a more contemporary color like pale rust, straw, or smoke. Import accent colors that complement the rug, the dishes you're hanging on the wall, or a favorite fabric. Judicious amounts of color or pattern—at the window, on a chair, or as a mat surrounding a print—will help unite all the elements. Carpeting—sisal being the most pleasing and inexpensive host of all—also pulls things together.

A more daring and dramatic approach would be to paint the walls a dark, rich color such as chocolate-brown and the trim a clean, crisp white. Against the dark walls, white-painted pieces with interesting shapes, black-and-white photographs in black frames, and furnishings upholstered in white shine. Elbow in a rattan chair, a wicker footstool, or a wooden trunk from India for texture. For windows, stick to natural cottons or natural fibers blended with synthetics for greater durability. Simple Roman or rattan shades are timeless and tasteful.

Once a comfortable sofa and chairs are in place, choose

Because all the elements gathered in this sun-washed room share the same relaxed attitude, they can all come contentedly together. The play of form, texture, and design origins only lends more spiciness. Rugs draped on the sofas supply a hint of color, while floors remain uncovered and light.

the supporting furnishings according to character. A 19th-century Spanish table and a set of American Empire chairs may not be a team anyone would normally think of, but try pairing them together. There's an old adage that holds if you buy only what you love, somehow it will all work—and it's true! Suspend an antique brass lantern over a glass-topped modern desk, and you've created your own moon over a waterlike tableau.

An eclectic-style room can incorporate the disparate possessions you've inherited as well as those vintage pieces you've collected. Assigning furnishings new roles is a tricky way to include pieces you like in

a small space. A chest of drawers, for instance, might double as a sideboard in a teeny dining room; a blanket chest or a pair of leather suitcases—one on top of the other—could fill in as a coffee table; a bedside table makes a nifty desk when you pull up a chair.

This balancing, yin and yang approach takes well to a kitchen where you want the warm, welcoming aura of home with professional-style appliances. It also works well in the bath where you hope not only to groom but relax. Fine hardwood cabinetry and high-style modern lighting? You bet. A glass-block shower and a fruitwood French armoire (to hide a tiny television as well as towels)? Absolutely. Forget the this-has-to-match cute notions of the past, and experiment. Jackie Kennedy's fashion advice to women was always to remove one thing from an outfit before going out. If you fear you've stirred the pot too much, do the same with your room; you might be amazed at the difference.

Traditional architecture steps back and allows some whimsy to happen—the orchids, the leafy curtains, a curved Gustavian-style bench, a bolster wrapped in beads! The combination of shapes and textures encompasses several styles successfully. Designer: Stacey Lapuk, ASID, CID

This room is the embodiment of eclecticism: old, metal outdoor chairs in their original paint teamed with an aged soda machine. Crowned with a tiled cement top, this sideboard has personality befitting a silver service.

GET THE LOOK
• Keeping proportion in mind, team a farmhouse table with new metal chairs.
• Stand a Lucite lamp on an antique desk.
• Mix sizes and framing styles for photographs and artwork.

Many people love fun, bright, irreverent retro style. Not assigned to any one decade, this is a look that calls in all of 20th-century design, including striking 1930s art deco as well as the fluorescent, psychedelic 1960s. Collectors and inveterate flea-market shoppers naturally gravitate to retro rooms that allow them to showcase their finds—everything from lava lamps to chrome chairs and garden gizmos. Sometimes more energized than organized, retro rooms have a sense of humor and a lot to say; after all, every object comes with a story of discovery. Sleek and chic or cottage charming, retro is fun to live with and fun to put together because it's whatever decade appeals to you.

The funky products of the '50s with their organic shapes and abstract patterns look right at home in a ranch house. These happy-day rooms—devoid of architectural trim and detail—take instantly to the hype of vinyl seat cushions and wacky flying-saucerlike lamps. Many of the '50s pieces have become highly collectible and increasingly hard to find, but mass-produced items can still be reasonably had at flea markets and consignment stores. Smaller, often overlooked items from the era such as game boards are stunning mounted on a wall; plant hangers in the shapes of fish are dynamite in a bath!

Neutral walls accommodate a tongue-in-cheek assortment of offerings. When quarters are tight, white or cream surfaces expand space. In a retro kitchen, glossy white cabinets, lots of shiny chrome counter edging, and stainless-steel appliances are a classic dish. Certain kitchen color teams—for example, black, red, and white—are reminiscent of the cozy intimacy of roadside diners. If your taste runs to colorful dinnerware though, a palette of Mexico-inspired colors throughout a room is for you. Look to your collections for inspiration. Art and furniture shapes can be enhanced with color. A pink-and-white plate or a pressed-glass cranberry compote could help establish the perfect palette.

Retro-patterned vinyl or linoleum flooring will enhance the freewheeling tone of a retro kitchen, family room, bath, or child's bedroom. Squares of black, red, turquoise, or yellow plus white have a lively jukebox kind of appeal everyone will like. Vintage rugs in geometric prints tossed over hardwood or carpeted floors will add some extra zing. When it comes to fabric for cushions, upholstery,

A 21st-century recipe brings homey details—the wall-mounted shelves filled with supplies, the pattern of vent holes in cabinets and counter—together with shiny stainless-steel appliances and hardware.

A retro dressing room demands some classy cabinetry, a glossy vanity with a glass top, plenty of chrome, and a mirror as big as the moon. The dashing contemporary lamp is a functional and catchy addition. **Architects: Mojo Stumer Associates**

and drapes, hunt up vintage (or reproduction) bark cloth. Available in endless colors and patterns (sputniks, tropical flowers, cowboys), woven bark cloth can give a room a sophisticated or kitschy edge. Keep drapes simple though, so as not to detract from all the other elements.

Lace doilies, vintage tablecloths strewn with sweet visions of flowers and fruit, straw hats, picnic baskets—these kinds of romantic items favor a retro 1940s cottage look. A tablecloth or scarf tossed over a simple wood rod becomes a curtain; a lacy tablecloth laid over a bed or a sofa is a heart-stopping bit of fantasy. If this sort of style leaves you weak in the knees, play it up with botanicals and samplers on the walls, old watering cans, decoupaged trays,

miniature houses, and lots of white wicker or white-painted furniture. Paint newer tag-sale bargains white, and then give them a crackle glaze to render them instantly older-looking and more endearing. Against white or pale, pale rose-pink or blue walls, the furnishings will seem as light as summer clouds.

Rotate collections to keep your room at the top of its form. In addition to open shelves, consider installing glass-front cabinets to hold smaller trinkets like dainty perfume bottles, salt and pepper shakers, and those things you've yet to find; there's always going to be a treasure around the corner.

GET THE LOOK

- Stay lighthearted with bright-colored tiles in kitchen and bath.
- Upholster footstools and piano seats with funky, wildflower patterns.
- Define a space or divide rooms with stylish glass block.

Love me tender, love me true, this upbeat room is as good as new. Very much in vogue, aluminum chairs and colorful dishes rock to the tune of a vintage jukebox. **Designer: Christina Waag**

Welcoming World Beat

Given modern travel and technology, our oceans have shrunk and the boundaries between nations have all but faded, and the result is a greater influx than ever of fresh and energizing ideas. Today you can celebrate a number of cultures without ever having to leave your home. A mix of elements—be they Asian, Swedish, or Indian—imbue a room with memorable presence and personality. You may already adore hurricane lamps, wooden shutters, tie-dyed fabrics, and vivid colors like azure and lemon-yellow and not know these elements have their roots in the Caribbean. Also, the dark Colonial-style furniture—much of it boldly carved—that is so coveted now was produced for British colonials who occupied the islands long ago. With a ceiling fan, some well-chosen rattan pieces, and a few large plants you can evoke a similar atmosphere without a lot of expense. Look beyond the styles you already are familiar with, and a whole world of breathtaking ideas awaits!

Far Eastern design inspires a serene setting where two can share a soothing cup of tea. The low table and soft floor pillows lend authenticity. **Architect: Robert D. Henry**

Materials that we have come to love such as bamboo, porcelain, lacquer, silk, and bronze, for instance, are all products of Asia, a country that has inspired architects and designers for centuries. Asia's refined furniture and fabric design had a dramatic effect on the Art and Crafts movement in the '30s. Military personnel who served in World War II, Korea, and Vietnam brought Asian furnishings home with them, and that also spurred American interest. Now, with most trade barriers down, many sought-after Asian pieces are readily available and affordable. A room derived from, say, a Japanese aesthetic provides a calming, Zen-like atmosphere, which is just what we need to relieve the stress of everyday pressures. For this kind of timeless decorating, a less-is-more approach works best. Since walls contain more square footage than any other surface in the room, wallcoverings are one of the simplest and quickest ways to infuse a living room or dining room with Asian ambience. Go global with patterns that mimic natural materials like bamboo, granite, and cork in subtle earth tones, or for more drama, investigate grass cloth or metallic grass cloth in copper or gold. Neutral-colored flooring such as sisal or sea grass rugs will allow your furniture to stand out and make your room appear lighter and airier than before.

A leopard frieze (the band along the top of the room) guards a space that has its roots in Africa. The animal-print fabrics and Colonial-style furniture are brought to life against the safari-mood wallpaper border. **Manufacturer: Brewster Wallcovering Co.**

To get a breath of Eastern air without scrapping all the furnishings and accessories in the room, invest in one wonderful piece. A shapely Japanese stair chest or an ornate antique Chinese table is better than a room full of minor players. To assure that your new star looks like it belongs, be sure to keep the scale consistent. Strip the space of accessories, and then carefully add back in ones that carry the right message. Minor alterations like changing the hardware on a hand-me-down bureau to metal handles inspired by characters of the Asian language will make a huge impact. And when it comes to flowers, do as the decorators do: A cache of graceful apple blossom branches or delicate yellow forsythia (you could force your own every spring) are far more enlightened in an Asian-inspired room than a fussy arrangement.

Moroccan and Indian accessories are very current and popular. Search out throws, floor pillows dazzling enough for a bedouin tent, and inexpensive but carefully chosen artifacts. Pretty Indian-inspired jacquard panels hung at the window or black-and-rust-colored hand-thrown pots from Tunisia exude an intriguing faraway flavor. Spice up your private domain, too. A reproduction Balinese bed mounded with velvet pillows and layered with a lush Moroccan brocade duvet and shams creates a scene right out of the Arabian Nights. Lay a hand-knotted rug from Turkey in

Originating in the mid-18th century, under the influence of King Gustav III, Scandinavian style is a look that slides effortlessly into place in a contemporary, open-plan house. Features that appeared long ago—delicate furniture, uncluttered rooms, and decorative paintings—are being embraced all over again. The spare lines and uncluttered, harmonious interiors address our need to slow down and appreciate life's little things, like the slant of the morning sun across a bare floor or the stillness that envelops a house when snow falls.

Born in a country deprived of the sun for months on end, Swedish style concocts a light of its own with rooms painted luminous shades of icy blue or muted white. Although these colors make up the classic recipe, you can achieve the same aura by painting walls (plaster or paneled) the palest grade of green or pink. A simple swag or a stenciled border of summer flowers trailing along a wall is traditional and adds visual interest in a living room, bedroom, or bath.

Southwestern architecture doesn't dictate the contents of this slate-floored, globally inspired room. The entertainment center exudes Indian flavor that is pronounced with a crimson-colored wall. The straw window shades and woven armchair are Asian imports. **Architect: Evan Eglin; Builder: The Kemmerly Company; Designer: Lori Carroll, ASID, IIDA**

mellow gold hues where your toes will find it first thing every morning.

Visit shops and galleries that specialize in imported furnishings as well as rugs and art. A lovely 20th-century kimono hung on the wall is an exotic accent. Design centers, home stores, furniture stores, and mail-order catalogs feature a large variety of tempting globally inspired furniture and accessories, everything from inexpensive hand-carved pagoda lamps and Chinese country baskets to lacquered Chinese-like storage units for books, CDs, tapes, and other media.

From the top of the world comes another design breeze with a similar pared-down and be-simple kind of attitude but with a whole different venue.

A classic Japanese tea ceremony or martinis for two? An East-meets-West room with a traditional low table, floor pillows, and garden view would suit both occasions.

Wallcoverings are also suitable, but they should be dainty in scale. Blue-and-white tiles (try a decorative ridge behind the kitchen or bath sink or around the hearth) are standard elements. Veto dark, gloomy wood floors in favor of light woods like beech or ash, or hide an existing floor under a coat of white paint. Curtains should be simple, unbleached muslin. If you can't live without a snap of color, gingham is pretty and also light-affirming.

Dark furnishings would upset the wintry mood, and nothing pulls together a mismatched group of furniture better than a coat of pristine white. One word of caution: Swedish rooms have few furnishings and what is used is carefully arranged around a focal point like a ceramic-tiled stove or fireplace. Edit what you have down to a few well-loved, comfortable pieces.

GET THE LOOK
• Cover pillows in crewel fabric or batik.
• Frame a large vintage world map for the dining or living room.
• Bleach floors and walls to shape a Scandinavian decor.

Scandinavian style is distinguished by clear colors, clean lines, and unfussy materials. It's a tasty recipe for a small, light-filled kitchen that wants to remain airy and open.

All these styles can come to life in your home. It's just a matter of making a few decisions and finding the right materials. When you walk into your house and smile, you know you've done it right.

Puzzle the Pieces Together

Close your eyes and you can see the room you want. Dressed with color and artfully arranged, it's just right. Now all you need to do is to make the dream a reality. Where to start? With the basics: walls, floors, ceilings, windows, and furnishings. Kitchens and baths will warrant extra attention when it comes to fixtures, surfaces, and appliances. And storage is never to be forgotten anywhere. Give your attention to each of these, and before you know it, you'll put together an extraordinary room—the very image of the one you envision—from top to bottom.

A classic blue and white scheme is guaranteed to please all ages all the time. Vintage light fixtures, a floor in keeping with the home's era, and monogrammed towels equal extra panache. **Stylist: Joetta Moulden**

On the Wall

There they are: bare walls waiting for you to transform them. Luckily, you've got an arsenal of possibilities. First, you'll want to consider how the room is used and how important a part you want your walls to play. Do you want them to fade away in the background or shout "look-at-me"? Do you prefer a stark, gallerylike air or a warm, let's-gather-around-the-piano kind of mood? How do you feel about paint, wallcoverings, and architectural elements? There are options in each category to support your decor. And, if your project entails more decoration than remodeling, you'll be amazed at the difference new wall treatments make.

Subtle old-world elegance is displayed in two complementary wallcoverings that share the same color range as the carpet. Paneling on the far wall helps lead traffic around the corner.
Designer: Sandpiper Studios; Distributor: Seabrook Wallcoverings

PAINT

Paint is the fastest, least expensive way to bring new life to dull walls. In just a few hours, it's possible to reinvent a room. Most experts recommend durable "eggshell" paint (with a slight sheen) for walls and semigloss paint for trim in homes without kids and pets. In more active households where fingerprints are a way of life, semigloss walls and high-gloss trim will endure the wear and tear and clean up better. The kind of paint you use, either oil or latex, really comes down to personal preference. New improvements in latex paints (water-based paints) have made them as durable and long-wearing as the oil-based variety. The main advantage of water-based over oil-based paints is that the former dry faster, emit less odor upon application, and clean up with water.

Remember: Light colors dry lighter and dark colors darker than how they appear wet. Paint-chip cards typically feature a half dozen light and dark variations of one color, making it easy to find complementary colors. You could choose a medium shade for your walls and the card's lightest shade for the trim. If the wall color appears too dominant, switch to a lighter value. Keep in mind: Dark colors will reduce the size of a room, making it cozier; pale colors will provide a sense of more space and light. Fallen in love with a bold flower pattern? Then you're going to want an equally strong background color to evoke the proper mood. Use the fabric's palette, and select either a dominant or secondary hue. For instance: For a warm atmosphere, paint walls the color of blossoms—orange, pink, yellow; for a cooler ambience, tone it down with walls the shade of subdued green leaves. To successfully forge a contrasting scheme, decorators generally advise sticking to three colors: a dominant color, a secondary color, and an accent color.

Dark trim cuts a room up visually, while liberal use of white trim brightens an intense color like red or cobalt blue. Contemporary-style rooms often exhibit walls and trim of the same color; traditional-style rooms usually feature white or contrast-color trim. Don't forget the ceiling! Dark colors will bring a ceiling down; light colors will create an illusion of height. If you're having trouble deciding on a ceiling color, revisit your paint card. Consider a color that is two shades lighter than your wall color. This maneuver blurs the delineation between walls and ceiling and will help make the room seem bigger. If you're working with a custom color, tinting the ceiling paint (if you're doing it yourself, look for "dripless" paint) one quarter of the color of your walls will produce the same effect.

If the Mediterranean is where you want to be, make it happen with walls that have been sponged and glazed the color of sun-warmed terra-cotta. Decorative paint treatments can establish a style, set a mood, provide texture, and hide flaws—all at the same time. Techniques range from simple color washes and glazes to add translucency to more complex processes like lacquering. No money left in the budget for marble? How about the faux variety? Many techniques like combing, ragging, stippling, and graining (which results in a woodlike effect) are

easy to master. Some of the more complicated methods such as marbling and tortoise-shelling will require a talented hand. Stenciling (buy patterns or make your own) often brings to mind Colonial homes and nurseries. But don't underestimate stenciling's potential for grown-up drama. In a Victorian bedroom, think about echoing a fabric or a wall-covering motif. Instead of a quiet border along the top of the living room wall, why not create a stenciled geometric design to lend an art nouveau flavor? Sometimes, combining a variety of techniques is interesting. For instance, an elaborate powder room could have color-washed walls stenciled to resemble wallpaper.

Wallcoverings

Want to wake up in a rose garden or read your daily paper in a book-filled library? Wallcoverings can make it happen. From novelty prints featuring rec-

Scenic wall murals ratchet up interest in a Colonial room filled with antiques. The windows are left mostly bare so as to not distract from the artful vistas. **Designers: Allen Ransome and Randall Vansyock**

In the 16th and 17th centuries, leather was often used in Europe for wall-hangings and table covers. Today, leather-covered tiles with whip stitching lend a modern room a sophisticated air. **Manufacturer: Artistic Tile**

you've always wanted—minus the cost of hiring an artist!

Gone are those fragile papers of the past. Many modern wallcoverings are washable and scrubbable, and that makes them suitable for kitchens and baths. And easing our burden, most manufacturers have set up their sample books with suggestions for colors, patterns, and textures that can be easily combined to create a custom look. For the best selection, visit home-improvement outlets, paint retailers, and design centers, and search the Web. Keep these pointers in mind:

- Small prints add visual interest and background color to open up a small space.
- Large prints or textural papers applied to a ceiling render a large room more intimate.

Adhering to the same color scheme but varying tile sizes and shapes is a good way to lend interest to bath walls. **Manufacturer: Artistic Tile**

ognizable objects like porcelains or urns (long a favorite with decorators for traditional rooms) to nostalgic patterns for contemporary spaces, there are literally hundreds of choices. Some wallcoverings replicate historical patterns and colors; others mimic faux-finishing techniques such as stippling and sponging. Currently very popular because they complement a variety of global decors are textile fibers, jute, and grasses.

If you don't want to take on the whole room, consider applying a border as a chair rail. Or use a colorful border to accentuate an interesting architectural feature such as a doorway or a fireplace. Borders that imitate crown moldings and other architectural details perk up lackluster rooms. And a scenic paper can give you that inspired mural

- Stripes and vertical prints appear to raise a ceiling; horizontal lines widen a room.

BUILT-IN APPEAL

If you've got a boxy, plain-Jane room, it's time to spruce it up. Take stock of what's there and what's not. Even though molding is commonly placed where the ceiling meets the wall, it can also be applied around windows and doors. Lumberyards generally stock a myriad of different moldings, many expressly designed for trimming windows. Changing the slender molding to wide, flat boards in a nondescript postwar house will help evoke a bungalowlike scene. Add ornately detailed moldings complete with carved corner blocks, and it'll shout "Victorian."

Crown molding brings an immediate infusion of character. But if your home is more laid-back, try marrying two strips of molding with wallpaper or stenciling in between. To shorten a wall, install a picture rail about 18 inches from the ceiling and then paint the wall above it the same color as the ceiling.

Baseboards come in various sizes and profiles and, in addition to adding stature, protect the bottom of the wall from scuffs. Walls lined with bookshelves are universally appealing. Wood paneling yields a snug, clubbish air when finished in a dark, rich hue or a beach-cottage ambience when whitewashed. Like many other wall-

coverings, paneling (available in sheets and premilled kits) also hides wall imperfections. Ready-made details usually of plaster, wood, or polymers, replicating elements found in historic homes as well as many updated versions, are also available. The plas-

Hang it up! Wall-mounted collections like this innovative grouping of handheld mirrors give new or old walls personality to spare. The framed black-and-white prints help to define the arrangement and interject rhythm.

tic adornments are more lightweight and well suited for a bath or kitchen because they're easy to clean and mildew-resistant. Look for ones that are prefinished in a variety of simulated wood grains and colors to match your particular style.

Interest Underfoot

Floors are on the front line of every good design. You'll want to choose yours with aesthetics and practicality in mind. Based on the style of your room, do you require a long-lasting hard surface that is made from a material such as wood or stone? Or would a resilient modern flooring material that marries good looks with easy care do the job? In general, lighter-colored flooring—no matter what it is—will make a room seem larger, and so will laying tiles on a diagonal rather than parallel to the walls. Hardwood floors last a lifetime and fit every decor. Favorite types include oak for country rooms; maple and cherry for traditional rooms; and beech, birch, and ash for contemporary spaces. Soft woods like pine exude down-home charm but don't hold up as well. Purists recommend natural oil treatments to protect wood floors from moisture and staining. But an impervious finish like polyurethane makes wood safe even for a busy bathroom.

Geometric and gorgeous! A patterned stone floor—in monochromatic colors—is all that's needed to offset the high drama of see-through glass tables and white-as-snow upholstery. **Architect: Angelo Luigi Tartaglia**

Along with natural wood-tone stains, wood floors can be color-washed with stains that let the grain show, painted a solid color, or decoratively painted; faux-stone combined with checkerboard squares are classic. Stenciling is another popular route, and spatter-painted wood floors (a solid-color ground flecked with dots of many different colors) were trendy in Colonial days and look surprisingly modern today. For the best results, floors should be repaired and sanded first.

Decorators praise wall-to-wall carpeting's ability to flow through a house and pull it all together. A home with an assortment of small rooms will look more expansive, even when window treatments and furnishings change from room to room, if the same carpet is used throughout. Carpet also provides insulation against noise and cold. But what will it be? All sorts of textures, colors, and costs are available (including many stain-resistant new blends). Natural matting made of materials like sisal and coir can be elegant or casual depending on the setting, furnishings, and accessories. However, natural coverings like these are tough on the feet and easily stained. To ensure years of service, look for carpets that are closely tufted or woven. A solid-colored carpet with a subtle pattern will have a more relaxed air. A patterned carpet—florals, checks, or stripes—is an energy boost for a bedroom or study.

Stone floors, such as marble, granite, slate, or limestone, are timeless when they are mixed with antiques or modern furnishings. What you give up in softness underfoot is more than made up for in beauty. Still, most require sealing to prevent staining and cost is a factor. To lower the price tag, choose granite (less slippery than marble) for the master bath, and carpet the bedroom. Or lay slate tiles in the entry and economical sisal down the hall.

Terra-cotta tiles made of fired clay are like chameleons in that they will take on whatever mood you wish. Have them installed in a traditional kitchen or a Southwestern family room. The tiles can be left as they are, sealed for more durability, or glazed to heighten their lustrous sunset color.

Solid-colored or hand-painted, ceramic tiles are also long-lasting and versatile. With hundreds of colors, patterns, sizes, sheens, and grout colors to choose from, don't relegate charismatic ceramic tiles to just the bath and kitchen. Transform the floor in a sunroom, dining room, or high-traffic family room.

Sheet vinyl or vinyl tile is affordable and, like ceramic tile, available in hundreds of colors and patterns. Everybody's favorite, black-and-white squares exude pizzazz in a retro kitchen or formal hall. Solid-color vinyl—vivid blue, say, like a tropical sea—is less popular but very effective in a bath or child's room. Realistic faux vinyls mimicking brick, granite, and terra-cotta tiles are also stylish.

Popular in commercial situations and comfortable to walk on, rubber flooring will lend a slick look to kitchens, laundry rooms, or mudrooms. Rubber flooring is also slip-resistant, which makes it great in a kids' bath. And inexpensive, hard-wearing linoleum is definitely back in a very big way. Made

from all-natural products, this flooring appeals to young designers who are discovering innovative ways to combine colors and patterns. Laminate flooring is a newer synthetic option that can look like marble, stone, or even distressed wood for a country room since the pattern is really a photograph of the real material. More durable than countertop laminates, this new flooring provides the look without the cost.

Don't forget that rugs of all sizes layered on top of any kind of floor can add comfort and interest, define sitting areas, or help plan a mood. For example, a floor cloth befits a Shaker kitchen, and a shag rug is perfect for a retro '50s den.

A marble mosaic floor is a dramatic presence in a very detailed library. Teamed with the stuccolike walls, it conjures up thoughts of an ancient Venetian palazzo. **Architect: David Estreich; Designer: Gail Green**

Dressing Windows and Doors

Portals to the outside world, windows and doors get plenty of attention so you'll need to dress them in a fashion appropriate to your style. Frame a view or go for privacy, either way the options are many, which means there's something for every room.

Window treatments impact the overall appearance of a space, but they also serve a practical purpose. While looking pretty or tailored, chic or country, these dressings help keep us warm in winter, cool in summer. Lightweight honeycomb shades, for example, do both. On a frigid winter night, wool or tapestry drapes pulled across French doors can also chase away the chills and imbue a family room with a pleasing cocoonlike mood. When the sun shines too brightly for napping or watching television, roll-up shades—on those same doors—stop the glare.

Combining elements is an easy way to get the look—and efficiency—you want. Simple, natural-colored matchstick blinds teamed with fabric panels is a flattering remedy, say, in a south-facing casual room. And when you don't relish giving up the light but crave privacy? Sheers teamed with blinds or ready-made pleated shades and simple curtains, gathered at either side of the window, are a good call. No longer white only, gossamer sheers are available in luscious hues like pale green and blue—with or without embroidery. In an elegant bedroom, pleated synthetic shades with the seductive look of silk and shantung will allow you to capture the sun and guard your privacy, especially if you choose shades that pull up from the bottom.

Wood blinds (with or without wood cornices), roller shades, and natural Roman shades in rattan or bamboo are easy companions for any room, whether modern, eclectic, or traditional, and they are a

Blue window shutters hark back to the classic Scandinavian design recipe of blue and white. Curtains would have seemed too fussy in conjunction with the streamlined furnishings and bare floor.

Café curtains are classic in kitchen or bath. Have them in crisp white cotton, or enliven them with colors or patterns. Fabric manufacturers are reinventing old favorites like stripes and checks in Caribbean hues such as watermelon, coral, and canary to give a kitchen bay a bright morning attitude.

Balloon shades, flowing draperies, swags, and jabots are ideal for a formal aura. Opulence, though, doesn't dictate expensive fabric and an elaborate presentation. A modest valance or panels of burlap (trimmed with a simple satin band to be more fashionable) hung on exposed black iron rods is in keeping with today's lean, but also sumptuous, decorating. Fashioned three times the width of the window, curtains made of simple, inexpensive material spell luxury!

Many newer homes feature large expanses of glass, magnifying issues of privacy and light control. For windows and patio doors like these, vertical blinds on a sliding track are a viable solution. Fashioned of materials such as linen, textured knits, or vinyl, these streamlined treatments are—with the tug of a cord—easily closed and opened. Some are also energy-efficient. In current colors like wheat, flannel, heather, and willow, the blinds complement a range of styles. A traditional drapery treatment will also work on a French door or slider as long as the rod extends well beyond the frame. Lace panels mounted on each door are charming in a French-style cottage manner. To highlight the

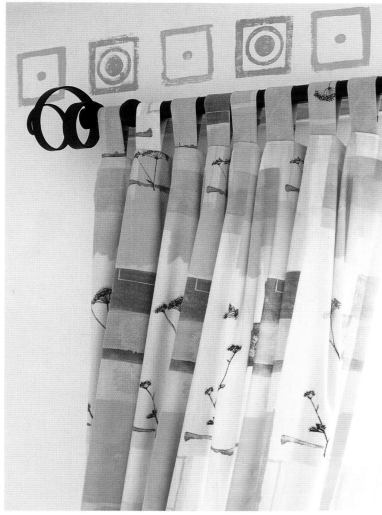

Black iron rods and simple tab curtains get a bang of excitement from free-wheeling finials. The finials' whimsical shape is happily in step with the bull's-eye wall stencil.

good choice when you're faced with a combination of windows and French doors. For privacy, natural Roman shades can be fitted with a liner on back. Many manufacturers offer fabric options for edge binding so you can coordinate the shade's binding with your upholstery for a custom look. These days, traditional wood blinds have updated optional twill tape patterns and 21st-century tape colors like persimmon, blueberry, and sable.

Asian-inspired screens diffuse the daytime light and provide privacy for a somewhat formal room that shuns anything too ornate. The Japanese-like sliding screens open to reveal the garden, which in Japan is considered another room.

window's operation, install blinds, shades, or inset curtains on each window.

Shop for hardware that will complement your window dressing. Fabric stores, home design centers, and catalogs are chock-full of decorative rods, finials, and holdbacks. Choices include modern nickel-plated cable rods for stylish urban settings and traditional polished brass rods with pineapple finials inspired by Williamsburg. A small detail, like a pair of beaded tassel holdbacks, will elevate inexpensive drapes to star status. Imagine what they would do teamed with soft velvet panels in your newly decorated living room!

shape of a window, a bank of windows, or a door, add just a top treatment such as a sculpted cornice or valance.

Use your window treatments to change the architecture. For example, extend treatments beyond a small window's frame to make the window look taller and wider. Drapes patterned with vertical stripes will appear to push the windows up and make the wall higher. Windows with challenging shapes—round or triangular—look best, though, with a simple dressing such as shirred fabric or a custom-fitted shade. If you have a Palladian-inspired semi-circular window above a window, one solution is to fix the rod at the bottom of the semicircle. Curtain the window below, and leave the arch above bare. Casement windows that open in rather than out are another problem. So as not to interfere with the

A sea captain's house welcomes whimsy. The painted door with its familiar scene of granddad and grandson scanning the horizon is in tune with the setting and also endearing.

The paint and wallcoverings are perfect. The window treatments are fabulous. But not until the furniture is moved in will the room be anything less than a pretty picture. You want sofas and chairs that beckon you home, dining chairs that persuade people to linger, and a bed that you'll hate to vacate. There's an outstanding supply of stylish, functional furnishings available in every price range, and they're all just waiting for you.

SOFT ESSENTIALS

Professionals warn: Never buy a major piece without knowing where it will go. Think about the role your room plays, and strive for furnishings to support it. For example, a child's room calls out for a comfortable and safe bed, a play table, and a chair. An active family room needs comfortable seating, a generous coffee table (if there's room, a 36-inch-square one is ideal) to hold magazines, and an assortment of side tables. In addition, an armoire or a wall unit will provide storage and a home for the television. But the antique rocker you envision can wait. Use your file and floor plan to help compile a list of the furnishings (along with their measurements) that you need right away to make your space livable. As time goes by, phase in the other elements. Better to buy a few quality pieces around which you can build your dream room rather than a truckload of this and that. You'll be able to afford high-quality pieces, too, if you fill in for the time being with budget-buys and proceed slowly. A well-constructed desk or chair, in the end, is a permanent plus. If you

In a sparse room every addition merits attention. A pine chest to hold towels and a free-standing mirror with ballerinalike feet are savvy counterpoints for a claw-foot tub. **Designer: Sallie Trout**

change houses or moods, the desk can move from the living room to a bedroom. If you're purchasing a sofa for a teenager's room, however, and don't anticipate wanting to keep it when he or she goes off to college, a less-expensive model will give you the look and save you money.

Formulating an arrangement on paper beforehand will afford a sense of how traffic patterns will work and where best to arrange a focal point. Begin with the largest piece. In a small sitting room, a love seat—combined with two upholstered chairs—is more flexible than an average-size sofa. Club chairs generally take up more footage than easy chairs, and dainty side chairs are easily shuffled wherever you need them. Every piece of furniture should be in proportion to the layout and to the other pieces. In front of a rustic fireplace, that could mean a three-cushion sofa across from a set of equally hefty armchairs. In a condominium, balance a plump sofa with a chair at either end; these chairs don't have to mirror one another, but to balance the design they should be visually compatible in heft and height.

Sofas and chairs with kiln-dried, hardwood frames and eight-way hand-tied springs are at the very top of the wanted-for-comfort-and-durability list. Prefabricated springs inserted into the frame are a moderately priced option. Side-by-side zigzag wires are the least comfortable but the most inexpensive. Cushion options range from down to popular, and less-pricey, polyurethane foam. Whatever your style, the more basic the lines and neutral the covering, the easier it will be to blend the piece with other furnishings. When you do finally tire of them, you will be able to reupholster or slipcover.

Thrift stores and flea markets sometimes yield unexpected upholstered treasures—everything from settees to contemporary wing chairs. However, if you're shopping for reproductions, do your homework first. Having some knowledge of period details helps. Reproductions are exact copies of antiques usually made with the same materials. Adaptations are looser in their interpretation of the original pieces in details and materials.

You could also check tag sales and consignment shops for furniture finds. Remember, though, before you purchase a piece of furniture that you plan to reupholster, examine its frame; if it also needs to be fixed, you could end up spending more money than you would on a new original. Still, if there is an emotional attachment (the chair is exactly like one your grandmother owned) or if it has wonderful details such as claw feet, the design may equal the expense.

The easiest and least costly makeover for salvaged pieces—and a great way to bridge a mishmash of furniture styles—are slipcovers. Make sure the chair is sound and the existing upholstery is in fairly good condition. A slipcover can turn the piece's look

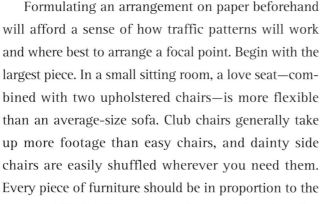

Furniture lends itself well to paint effects. Here, a subtle graining technique enhances a large bookcase's lines and helps provide a proper setting for art objects and old, leather-bound books.
Designers: Dan and Judy Mulligan

around, but it can't make it comfortable. Look for pieces with clean lines and strong shapes for best results. Slipcovers cover the whole gamut of styles, including country, traditional, and modern. Choose luxurious or textured fabrics such as brocade, velveteens, or chintz for a formal living room. In a country casual space order medium-weight cottons, linens, and cotton and linen blends. Natural fibers fit today's pace because they're easy: Throw them in the washer after your daughter's birthday party, and pop them back on while they're still slightly damp for the best fit. Combining fabrics—denim on the chair's back, for example, and a more expensive paisley on the front and sides—is a tricky way to save money and use the fabric you love. This mix-and-match technique suits most sofas and chairs and works for both slipcovers and upholstery.

Wondrous Wood

A room full of only upholstered pieces would be as dull as dishwater. Nonupholstered furniture, such as a 19th-century wood writing desk, help to make a well-dressed room. New or old wood furniture is constructed of either a hardwood like maple or oak or a soft wood like pine. Veneer is a thin layer of wood bonded to a heavier surface of a lesser-quality wood to make it look like cherry, for instance, or walnut. Many new pieces are made of veneer construction. Check the hangtag for a list of which woods or veneers were used. And be sure the piece is sound and the finish smooth. Good dining chairs and tables, for instance, will have corner blocks at the joints for greater stability. Sideboards should have doors that swing freely; dressers should have drawers that glide without sticking. It's perfectly acceptable and actually advisable to mix wood with

rattan or iron or to blend different kinds of wood together in one room. For example, birch veneer cabinets and a sideboard painted dark green would suit a handsome Arts and Crafts kitchen.

Refinishing, like upholstery, adds up unless you take the task on yourself. Paint is faster and less pricey. Paint a stodgy turn-of-the-century dining set white and add some bright, checked, tie-on cushions and a wiry plant stand full of colorful potted geraniums to transform your dining room into a garden. In a small bedroom, painting a big bed white against light-colored walls will help minimize the bed's size. Pile on the toile pillows, and it's a Parisian lair!

Faux bamboo-style table and chairs keep this Scandinavian-inspired breakfast area looking bright and light. Set on a dark-tiled floor, the furnishings almost appear to float. **Designer: Joseph P. Horan, FASID**

Heavy pots that boil over, greasy pans, sticky cosmetics! The life of countertops and backsplashes is fraught with peril. And on top of their hard work and long hours, these highly visible surfaces are expected to be good-looking. Their color, pattern, and texture will help determine your room's look. Find the right materials to suit your needs and style, and the payback will be years of dedicated service and beauty.

COUNT-ON-ME COUNTERTOPS

The counter where you prepare meals, where the kids set their homework, and where friends prop their elbows during those long heart-to-heart talks can help influence the way your kitchen feels and looks. Glass, granite, and other reflective materials intensify natural light. Shiny surfaces such as those made from polished granite will brighten a small, dark room. To cozy up a large kitchen, on the other hand, order a rougher material with a low-luster honed finish. Another idea, especially helpful if you're watching costs, is to mix materials: Choose a less-expensive alternative for the countertops, and insert a slab of marble for rolling pie dough. In any case, before you make a decision, consider the following:

- Natural stone, such as marble, granite, and slate, is the most expensive and luxurious. Its age-old appeal suits traditional rooms or high-end contemporary settings. A rose-colored marble top, for instance, would lend a note of sophistication to a traditional cherry bar. Sultry, gray granite would complement impeccably designed maple cabinetry in a modern kitchen. Contrasting colors—dark wood with light stone—bring attention to each.

- Wood is a handsome staple in country and traditional kitchens. But because the material is suscep-

Who wouldn't want to perch here? Polished granite makes an inviting, workable surface for the furniturelike island. Granite on either side of the range is handy for the cook. **Manufacturer: Brass Light Gallery**

Granite, a luxury choice for this island, will last a lifetime. Durable ceramic tile on the counters also resists stains, water, and heat, and will prove as practical as it is beautiful. Hand-painted flower tiles evoke spring thoughts for the cook even in the midst of winter.
Architect: Frank Glynn; Cabinetry: Robert F. Mattice; Designer: Judy Campbell, ASID

tible to warping and cracking if exposed to water, countertops are typically made of butcher block, which consists of many small wood pieces glued together. Since wood is porous, it should be regularly cleaned with an antibacterial cleaner. A polyurethane finish will increase the wood's sheen and life.

- Ceramic tile has long been a favorite due to its versatility and affordability. Liable to chip or crack if someone drops a weighty dish, however, tile is more likely to be used as a secondary work surface. For example, tile would be a good choice for a breakfast counter. Tiles in many colors and patterns afford endless opportunities for being creative and staying on budget.

- Solid surfacing is extremely long-wearing, non-porous (won't trap germs), and easy to repair. Best of all, solid surfacing allows for an integral sink that blends seamlessly with the countertop, a great boon for a busy family where daily upkeep is a chore. Colors vary from snowy white to rich caramel and copper-colored faux-stone to give a contemporary or eclectic room a jolt of elegance—minus the cost.

- Laminate, the most popular choice for kitchen and bath countertops, is available in hundreds of easy-

A reflective metal tile backsplash—in an offset tile pattern— imbues the cooking area with some light-catching glitter. The tile's silvery look ties in with the steel appliances and the suspended glass shelving.
Designer: Kirsten Cavan and Anna Marie Madsen

BENEFICIAL BACKSPLASHES

Be an artist. A few hand-painted ceramic tiles (your favorite herbs, fish, flowers?) scattered on a sea of manufactured tiles set a theme for an entire room. Diamond-shaped tiles are fun as accents. And tiles that resemble quarried stone and terra-cotta are dynamite in a rustic kitchen or a Craftsman-style kitchen. Use ceramic tile to create a focal point: tile behind the range as well as along the rim of the range hood. Combine matte and glossy tiles for added personality. Want something graphic? Dark grout will give pale tiles an interesting gridlike appearance.

BATHING BEAUTIES

Organic materials are ideal for a soothing, at-home spa. Honed sandstone, travertine, and limestone provide texture and depth in neutral tones for countertops and floors. More glamorous granite and marble can deliver a Roman bath persona particularly if the tub and floor wear the same material. A furniture-style vanity could become a European washbasin with a dove-colored marble top and backsplash. To transform your walk-in shower into a romantic grotto, consider dark-colored ceramic tiles or, to foster a sense of luxury and to keep you within budget, ceramic tiles resembling tumbled marble and quarried stone. Glass blocks—as a window or shower wall—usher in light but maintain privacy.

to-clean waterproof colors and patterns. The one drawback is that, since the color doesn't go all the way through, nicks and cuts will eventually show.

- Concrete allows you to stain or texturize your countertop to coordinate with cabinets and flooring. A good buddy for stainless steel, cement holds its own in a contemporary setting.
- Other options include shiny, hygienic stainless steel—ideal for dedicated cooks who covet a restaurant ambience—and glass. A quarter-inch-thick glass counter is dramatic and easy-care.

Cabinets are one of the most prominent elements in a kitchen or bath. To a great extent, the look of your room will be determined by their style, material, and finish. Unfortunately, according to experts, cabinets will also gobble up a significant chunk of your budget. Rather than buy new cabinets, an easy solution is to refinish, reface with laminates or wood, or reinvent existing cabinets with architectural trim, new hardware, or a decorative paint treatment. If none of these will do, the market holds lots of choices.

Custom cabinets are designed and built for your kitchen; semicustom cabinets are made primarily of stock components but have various options like decorative moldings and etched-glass door inserts; and, the least costly, stock cabinets are mass-produced to standard size specifications. There are numerous varieties of styles and materials, but just two basic construction types. Modernists will connect with frameless, or Euro-style, cabinets. These units have doors that are flush with the outer edge of the cabinet box, which gives them a slick contemporary appeal. This construction is ideal for laminates or veneer. Face-framed cabinets have rectangular frames that strengthen the cabinet boxes and provide a place to mount doors. With more detailing on the doors, face-framed cabinets are traditional. Raised panels, say, are classic fares. Construction materials vary, but the majority of cabinets are constructed from plywood or composite-board boxes covered with wood veneers. Some companies offer metal doors, and some vinyl doors replicate traditional panel styles.

Abundant cabinetry equals organization in a kitchen designed for entertaining. To allow easy access to the dining area, install glass-front cabinets to float over the counter. **Manufacturer: Brass Light Gallery**

A cherry finish with a chocolate glaze brings out the beauty of these wood cabinets. Designed for storage and display, the cabinetry includes niches for pretty glassware and openings for baskets.
Manufacturer: Wellborn Cabinet, Inc.

Popular options for finishes include any number of wood tones and light, pastel glazes. White or light cabinetry expands space—a great help in mini-kitchens—and can be formal or casual. A simple wood veneer like cherry or maple will heat up a stark setting. Mixed finishes—some painted cabinets, for instance, along with some chicory-glazed birch cabinets—cook up a kitchen that is unique and inviting.

Many manufacturers also offer furniture-style pieces such as hutches and pie safes as part of their lines. Consider including one of these in a different color or a distressed finish for a country appeal. A combination of glass- and solid-door cabinetry is a refreshing change for the eye and helps keep any room looking more open. Glass fronts also allow you to find what you need in a hurry.

STORAGE BOOSTER

There's no such thing as too much storage. Especially in a modern setting, clutter is a no-no. To help forge a niche for everything in the two busiest rooms in the house, adopt one or more of these strategies:

• Instead of wasting valuable space with a soffit, zoom extra-tall above-counter cabinets to the ceiling. Use this space for storing seldom-used serving dishes in a kitchen and surplus supplies in the bath. Put deep, narrow spaces to work holding pan lids, cookie sheets, or a foldable drying rack.

• Incorporate a series of shallow drawers for spices and silverware. Pullout drawers beneath the cooktop can corral pots and pans. Pullout pantries and lazy Susans deliver what you need without making you rummage. Generous drawers work for stashing unsightly garbage and recycling bins.

- Use appliance garages with sliding, hinged, or tambour doors to hide the microwave, coffee-maker, and toaster. In the bath, designate a pullout drawer for the hair dryer.

BRING IN THE OLD

Old furniture—be it an antique of 100 years or a character-filled piece from the '30s—provides a special flourish for a bathroom or kitchen. Trendy now in our country, this marrying of new and old is common in Europe. In lieu of an island, how about a marble-topped table or, in a small country kitchen, a countertop of old butcher block? Food preparation, buffet service? A vintage piece does it all.

Find a handsomely patinated table, and have it fitted with a shelf. Store baskets of linens or cookbooks there. Or leave it shelfless, so you can pull up chairs and stage an informal, spur-of-the-moment

Straightforward cabinetry painted white expands the dimensions of a teeny bath and affords nooks and crannies for all the necessary grooming accoutrements. Where space is limited, think tall! Nifty cone-shaped light sconces also help pull the design upward.

dinner with friends. Like new cars, modern vanities dazzle us. But for something no one else will have, look to the past. An auction-bought oak dresser, given a hand-painted sink and a polyurethane sealer, will be reborn as the belle of the bath.

When it comes to appliances, you really can have it all. Today's products are stylish, hardworking, and environmentally in tune. There are models for every pocketbook and style. Don't settle for anything less than exactly what you want. Heed the experts' advice, and research the newest developments before you sign on the dotted line.

Everyday Workhorses

Soup's on—but on what? The traditional range or stove combining a cooktop above with an oven below is an affordable, space-saving solution for many households. However, serious chefs are drawn to commercial-style (or sometimes actual restaurant-grade) stoves. With six or eight burners, basting and grilling functions, and built-in warming ovens, these gems are an incentive to cook. Not only that, in addition to stainless steel, the stoves come in savory colors such as eggplant, lemonade, and mint julep.

Modular cooktops that let you add features such as griddles, steamers, and rotisseries are also popular. These days, a modular approach to kitchen design allows people to better plan how they want to cook. For example, one wall oven near the island, another on the other side of the room for items that require less monitoring; or a gas cooktop in the island and an electric oven under the counter. Look for appliances that do several jobs such as wall units that offer the convenience of a microwave, a warming drawer, and a convection oven all in one but fit in the same space as a standard-size double oven.

Range hoods—in commercial-chic stainless steel, copper, tile, or country-mode wood—enhance a decorating scheme while funneling cooking odors and vaporized grease to a fan. For maximum effective-

A cooktop with smooth top burners partners efficiently with an under-the-counter range in matching black. The shiny black appliances complement the Euro-modern kitchen's gleaming tile, countertops, and molding. **Manufacturer: DACOR**

ness, a hood should be the same width as the cooking surface. But aside from that, the sky's the limit. Pair a richly carved wood range hood with traditional cabinets that sport arched cathedral doors, or combine a super-modern copper range hood with blonde wood cabinetry and glass counters for a Euro-style look.

Refrigerators have felt the commercial styling trend, too. Stainless-steel exteriors are featured in a wide range of prices and sizes. Consumer-friendly options include tilt-out storage drawers, deep-in-the-door bins, and pullout shelves. Auxiliary refrigerators are also helpful: stand-alone ice-maker units, wine refrigerators, and refrigerator drawers that look like cabinets but reveal a freezer or refrigeration unit. Does your household include hungry kids? A convenient pullout refrigerator drawer for snacks, a microwave situated below the counter, and an area of lowered counter space will keep them out of your work zone and satisfied.

Dishwashers are practically silent these days, and federal guidelines ensure they're energy-efficient. Some models have sensors that tell them when dishes are clean so no energy is wasted heating extra water. Available from domestic and foreign manufacturers, some models are streamlined like race cars.

If you don't relish the standard white, black, or stainless-steel finish for your appliances, manufacturers offer coordinated cabinet fronts for a very custom-designed look. When the work is done and the kitchen is quiet, it will be hard to decipher your tools from the cabinets!

CREATE A WORK TRIANGLE

In order for a kitchen and cook to function best, a good floor plan must be in order. The work triangle—an important element in kitchen design for years—describes the relationship of the three major work areas: refrigerator, cooking source, and sink. If you draw an imaginary line from the sink to the cooktop to the fridge and back to the sink, it should form a triangle. With the diversity of appliances out there and with families cooking together, however, variations can also work. Two cooks, for example, could share the fridge with separate work stations adapted to their needs.

The National Kitchen and Bath Association has put forth guidelines for planning a work triangle:

- Each leg of the triangle should measure between four and nine feet long.
- The 3 legs' total length should equal between 12 and 26 feet.
- Traffic patterns shouldn't interfere with the triangle.
- Cabinetry shouldn't intersect any triangle leg by more than one foot.

MAKE LIFE EASY

Kitchen designers and manufacturers are doing their best to give us a helping hand. Have you thought of incorporating a pot spigot by the stove to fill unwieldy pots there instead of lugging them across the kitchen? A piping-hot water dispenser would mean no more standing around waiting for the pot to boil for tea. Full-slide drawers that afford you an overall view—even those distant corners—facilitate organization. And when everybody's late again? Don't fret. A warming drawer heats up plates and keeps dinner warm and moist until you're ready. On a higher level still, technology companies and appliance manufacturers are joining together to create a whole new generation of "smart appliances" to be controlled via the computer. From water faucet to oven, click on and tell them what to do!

High performance in a compact kitchen translates top-notch fixtures and appliances along with a marble island that features a flip-up steel countertop when extra work space is required.
Manufacturer: Kohler Co.

Storage and Shelving for Elsewhere in the House

A generous amount of storage keeps every home looking cleaner and neater. Take advantage of every nook and corner. If you're using boxes or baskets that hide what's inside, label them. And don't allot any items—CDs, clothes, toys—more room than is necessary. New homes today have about three times as many closets as houses built in the '50s, but it seems that's still not enough. Here are some ideas to help you find a place for everything:

- **Collect Cabinetry:** When storage is an integral part of the architecture, the sense of orderliness is enhanced. Instead of simply placing some shelving on the family room wall, for instance, transform the entire wall into a storage area made of continuous materials. The latest trend is to use cabinetry as furniture in home offices, master suites, and bedrooms. In addition to making room for electronic gear, papers, and books, the cabinetry, complete with doors and niches, creates a consistent, pleasing picture. Be sure to research the hundreds of cabinetry choices, and choose a style that will help to provoke the look you want. Styles include a variety of woods that can be stained, glazed, or painted. In a period dining room, a wall of detailed cabinetry in a rich wood tone would set an old-world mood. Include a glass door or two, and let your prettiest china show. Use wood or laminate cabinetry in a home office. But leave the midsection open as a desk to hold the computer.

To fashion a berth for surplus china and to separate the dining area from the cooking zone, think about a room-divider cabinet. When company comes to dinner, use the top of the cabinet as a serving station. A cabinet like this is also a good way to divide a bedroom for kids. Paint the cabinet a different color on each side, and include an even number of shelves for each child.

- **Move in Modulars:** Modular units are available in dozens of styles and materials from plastic to wood. Assemble a wallcovering configuration in the den, the home office, or a child's room. Flanking a window or arranged on either side of a bed, twin units become receptacles for books and family photographs. Look for "towers" and horizontal cabinets that can be stacked in order to take advantage of vertical space.

- **Find Functional Furniture:** Furniture designers know consumers want furniture that

A contemporary shelving unit takes advantage of a large niche created by this room's architecture. Flush against the wall, glass shelves securely hold fragile art objects as well as books.
Architect: Angelo Luigi Tartaglia

It's a hectic workday morning, but this lucky man can see exactly what he needs. Tidy shirt shelves and a tie cupboard—all part of some very well-planned closet cabinetry—make putting clothes away and dressing a snap.

functions on a practical and an aesthetic level. A chocolate-stain-and-lacquer-finished media cabinet would be a handsome addition to a traditional or contemporary room. But with a generous drawer for organizing videos and music, it's even more welcome.

In addition to classic old-fashioned hardwood bookcases, there are freestanding sculptural shelf units manufactured in retro modern shapes and materials like polypropylene and aluminum. Stylish in themselves, these kinds of units make a convenient and chic display for artifacts or books. Also available are sculptural side tables constructed to corral magazines and newspapers. Parked along-

side a pair of modern easy chairs, such artful tables will gather attention no matter if they're empty or filled.

• **Commission a Carpenter:** Use those corners! In the bedroom, design a Craftsman-style angled cupboard (with doors) to hold the television. Add two comfy chairs, and you have a private just-for-two spot for watching the news. Hide a tiny bar fridge behind those doors, and you can have a drink or snack without having to traipse to the kitchen.

Open shelves are another excellent way to maximize wasted corner space. Line a corner with glass shelves in the bath, and display your daintiest toiletries. Open shelves will also work in the space beneath a stairway.

Add a window seat with lift-up top (underneath a decorative cushion) in the family room or kitchen breakfast area. Stash linens or extra blankets (who will know?) inside.

Fashioning an entire wall of storage renders a room more intimate in addition to providing storage. Here, a library ladder is ready to roll whenever it's needed. **Manufacturer: Putman Rolling Ladder Co., Inc.**

If you're remodeling a bath, real luxury translates room for two: twin vanities, a separate enclosure for the shower and the tub, and a toilet isolated in its own compartment. Simply replacing a worn-out fixture or an out-of-date faucet, though, is enough to give a bath or kitchen a shot in the arm. Not anticipating taking on the entire room or relocating plumbing means more money to buy products that speak to you. Top-of-the-line hardware, a hand-held shower, or a steam bath? The market is flooded with creature comforts.

FIXTURES AND FAUCETS

Who doesn't need a stress reliever by the day's end? Enhance a whirlpool tub (remodeled units fit right into a standard tub recess) with accessories like a hand-held sprayer or a cascading faucet. Design a custom walk-in shower finished with easy-to-clean ceramic tile or glass block. A massaging showerhead will chase away workout and stress-related aches and pains. Pamper yourself. Pile on the fluffy towels and the perfumed soaps! Decorate for all the senses as well as the eye.

Pedestal and wall-hung sinks are traditional fare. But a modern pedestal sink can also be lean and sculptural—a worthy partner for slick surfaces. A sink with Queen Anne-style legs would infuse a spacious bath with European elegance. So would a wall-mounted towel warmer and a heat lamp.

Counter sinks, generally of vitreous china, can be dropped in or mounted onto virtually any kind of counter. Self-rimming sinks rest on top. Simple,

The seductive curve of a polished chrome faucet is replicated by a curvy soap dispenser. Offset with metal sinks and ocean-blue tile, the look is as cool as a sea breeze.

graceful bowls of, say, art glass or metal appear to float. A glass bowl atop a stone counter creates a harmonious play of light and texture. Integral sinks, manufactured from solid surfacing, fuse seamlessly with the countertop and are very popular in high-traffic situations.

What to consider in choosing style and color? Dramatic dark colors may be less likely to show dirt. But, they're easily marked with soap scum and hard-water mineral deposits. Neutral shades adapt to all color towels and accessories and, if this isn't your dream house, will most likely please new buyers. In general, simple is better in everything from fixtures to faucets. Fancy scrollwork and doodads can make the latter appear quickly dated. Instead, use shapes and forms to help get your look across. Brass is the standard faucet base material, but manufacturers offer an array of finishes including nickel, copper, and chrome for all kinds of styles including those high-arched faucets with built-in sprayers designed to take on any kind of challenge.

Kitchen sinks have revved up their personalities, too. A heavy-gauge copper farmhouse sink recalls the days when every butler's pantry had a copper sink for washing delicate glassware. A roomy apron-front soapstone sink is understated and timeless. Don't skimp on accessories here either. Cutting boards, wire rinse baskets, and colanders can ease chores as well as provide stylish details.

HARDWARE

Hardware—cabinet knobs and handles, drawer pulls, and window cranks—doesn't have to match. But for uniformity, limit the number of different finishes and colors to a minimum of two or three, particularly if hardware is visible in the front entrance or an adjoining family or great room. Classic types of hardware like wood and brass knobs never lose their appeal. But new hand-forged metal knobs and porcelain shapes—leaves, arrows, fish—are intriguing and eclectic. Maybe you could find something from a local artisan who specializes in handcrafted hardware. If you're rejuvenating rather than remodeling a kitchen or a bath (or a piece of furniture), replacing the hardware—or adding hardware where none has previously existed—is one of the quickest and easiest fix-ups you can do.

As a general rule, antiqued brass, nickel-finish steel, and wrought iron are considered traditional; shiny steel and chrome are modern. But shape also counts in how the hardware comes across. And

clever substitutions are appreciated: for instance, rope pulls in a log cabin, Mexican concha buckles in a Southwestern dining room, seashells for the vanity in an island hideaway. In the same way a certain piece of jewelry can turn an outfit around, hardware matters.

Ideas for small details like hardware or for whole decorating schemes surround you all the time. Everywhere you look, everything you read, the trips you take—it's all inspiration. Keep adding to your files. To help, we've assembled some ideas of our own in the chapter ahead.

Washing up takes on new meaning when the sink is a multi-colored glass bowl floating on a fused-glass countertop. A low-key faucet helps focus attention on what's happening below.
Manufacturer: Alchemy Glass & Light

Decorating Ideas

From foyer to family room, every corner of your home should signal your personality as well as be comfortable and efficient for your family. Don't be daunted by empty rooms or tight budgets. A stark kitchen that suits one couple leaves another cold. Lavish chintz drapes would please a staunch traditionalist but never do in a minimalist's retreat. Start with what you love: your favorite colors, furnishings, art, and accessories. Then look to the useful tips and advice here to help you achieve your own individual decorating style. Home is where the heart is; just follow yours and you won't go wrong.

Decorating needs to come from within. To a backdrop you love, add furniture, textures, and patterns to make every room a special space. A classic blue-and-white combination allows dark furniture to show off its lines. Details—from the lush comforter to the porcelain—add notes of undeniable sumptuousness.

Lovable Living Rooms

Maybe there was a time when living rooms were roped-off areas consigned to special occasions only. But many 21st-century living rooms are used every day. In newer homes, in fact, living and dining areas often merge with the kitchen. Round-the-clock hubs, these versatile open spaces allow for any number of activities to take place simultaneously. Unlike those antiquated "family rooms" from the past that were defined as a recreation room in the basement with a pool table as the highlight, today's family hangouts are apt to feature a sophisticated media center and a handsome built-in bar complete with under-the-counter fridge and microwave. There might even be a wine cellar next door to facilitate entertaining.

On the other hand, some homes provide additional rooms that can be set aside for primarily adult gatherings. Either way, fabrics, furnishings, and accessories can turn the level of formality up or down. Floor-to-ceiling panels topped with valances, Oriental carpets, and antiques are traditionally gracious. However, in a

contemporary setting, an equal degree of polish is gained with

smart linen-covered sofas, understated window treatments, and a

sea-grass carpet. A fireplace, French doors, or a handsome enter-

tainment center can be dubbed the focal point around which you

arrange a series of comfortable chairs and easy-to-move tables.

If the be-careful-where-you-touch persona isn't for you, incor-

porate durable nylon or cotton fabrics and patterns that mask stains. Overstuffed rolled

arm sofas with comfy pillows and club chairs are less formal than those pieces with clas-

sic lines such as camelback sofas. Sturdy furniture designs like Windsor chairs are more

unassuming than shield-shaped

chairs. And slouchy slipcovers

that can be popped in the washer

are more family-friendly than

upholstery. To lighten the tone of

a classic room vary wood fin-

ishes, add a mismatched chair, or, for an exotic note, include a bamboo table. Smooth textures like gleaming wood, glass, and lacquer tend to be formal. Rougher textures such as sisal carpet or Adirondack furniture are more casual. An eclectic room will include a savvy mix of fabrics and furniture styles that play off one another; for instance, a dark Victorian carved mirror ascending over a modern glass table.

Include multiple-personality pieces like ottomans, benches, and carts to make a room flexible. A cart that holds cocktail-making supplies on Saturday night can also tote books or weekday snacks for the kids. A painted bench is a seat, a magazine holder, or a shelf for flowering plants.

If built-ins aren't an option, modular furniture systems offer a tempting variety of cube and shelf components with which you can create storage walls, towers, entertain-

ment centers, and desks. A vintage or new baker's rack or a dresser with open storage up top also provides a character-filled display. Stackable tables, light-weight folding chairs, TV trays like our parents had, drop-leaf tables, and floor pillows that slide away under a sideboard when not needed suit family life as well as crowds.

When night descends, switch on a medley of lights to warm the room and lift the spirits of all who enter. It isn't necessary that lamps flanking a sofa or guarding a mantel match, as long as they are of a

similar mood and visual weight. And don't be limited by your home's history; contemporary lighting is a fascinating counterpoint for an old house. Install spotlights to illuminate artwork and other focal points and dimmers to set a we-love-staying-home ambience.

Never mind the time of year or the weather, this living room has taken color to heart. Red, yellow, and blue upholstery injects the cream-colored setting with beguiling warmth. With such vibrancy all around, little else is needed. Chosen for their form as well as their comfort-factor, the chairs, love seats, and sofa are upholstered minus skirts or ruffles. This is a strategy that helps to keep the room feeling open and clean. Rather than focus on the fireplace, the seating arrangement turns its attention inward to the amiable glass table. The shape of the window is mimicked by the straight backs of the furniture and also by a stylish room divider directly opposite the room. Reminiscent of a Japanese screen with its panels of frosted glass, the divider subtly separates the entry hall from the sitting area. To allow the exotic flavor of the furnishings to dominate, accessories are limited. A piece of sculptural glass and a cone-shaped lamp serve as extra sparks in a room that proves, once and for all, that contemporary needn't be cold.

Left: *Touches of cobalt blue—replicating the blue of the sofa seen in the other photo—lead the eye around the room. Interesting shapes—note the curvaceous arms on chairs—and a few pieces of bold art highlight the room.*
Right: *Symmetry—dual golden chairs and a pair of love seats—adds harmony to the striking scene. Built-in niches flanking the fireplace have the same effect. The coffee table affords every guest a spot to set down a drink, and it doesn't appear cumbersome due to its see-through top.*

Architects: Mojo Stumer Associates

eticulous cherry millwork in this mountain retreat is a reminder of the emphasis the Arts and Crafts style placed on craft. Natural warm colors and high-quality but informal materials were the mandate. Here, the warm-hued wood and the stonework fabricated of local Idaho quartzite (a metamorphic rock consisting essentially of quartz in interlocking grains) create a similar look for a great room where skiers gather. The comfortable furnishings also speak to the style. In the kitchen area, which remains in full view of the hearth, and in the entry, cherry wood cabinetry continues the mood. Even the light fixtures are reminders of the period's tenet to combine the useful with the beautiful. At night, pools of soft light—some even spilling from the cleverly placed second-story interior window—illuminate the millwork and make it more lustrous still.

Left: *With plentiful seating for all, this hearth is likely the family's favorite meeting place. The sliver of a mantel allows space for favorite photographs without distracting from the beauty of the natural stone.*

Right: *An Arts and Crafts sensibility awards everything a storage spot, so no matter how large the crowd, the room stays neat. Glass-front cabinets help bring light into the kitchen.*

Architect: Coty N. Sidnam/Sidnam Petrone Gartner Architects

Casual Chic

A shiny white layout such as this might have come across as too sterile. But these smart owners warmed up their great room with upholstery that brings the garden inside all year long. A soft area rug, mounds of puffy pillows, and warm-toned wood furnishings offset the bare glass and shiny floor in the dining section. In addition to the red-brown bricks of the hearth and the luxurious L-shaped window seat, cozy touches include art, flowers, candles, and family photographs. The close proximity of the kitchen to dining and living areas makes the space seem intimate and is ideal when family and friends assemble. The stools slide out of the way, and the kitchen counter becomes the serving station for a turkey dinner or something as simple as crowd-pleasing chips and dips. Thanks to the well-planned architecture, family members can pursue different activities—like reading, watching the news, and cooking—and still share time together.

Above: *A sofa with a curved shape is a gentle barrier between the rest of the room and the sitting area. The table behind the sofa also contributes a feeling of separation without being too obvious.*

Opposite: *Cleverly opening the wall at the base of the window seat prevents that corner from being shut off from the rest of the room. A wall of cabinetry makes a fine home for the TV.*

Architect: Ray Spehar; Designer: Eric Mitchell Shore Design; Manufacturer: Charlie Hallam

Below: *The step-down design of the entry—complete with massive pillars—is a dramatic preview for the room beyond. Pairing bricks with wood is also a method to increase interest. Smaller details—the cowhide-upholstered chair and the iron table lamp—add to the delight.*

Architecture is the jumping-off point for this intriguing living room's decor. The creamy stucco walls and the wood-covered ceiling are traditional in the Southwest. The visual weight of the beams suggests a vernacular that has endured for centuries with very few changes. In order to allow the character of the room to reign, furnishings needed to be straightforward, unpretentious, and minimal. To offset the chocolate-brown upholstery and the rich leather chairs, bright Navajo rugs and green plants are all that's required. Accents of black iron hark back to the Spanish influence in the area. Best of all, the interesting armoire doesn't give a clue it's hiding electronics so, when the doors are closed, the ambience remains undisturbed. The owners might enjoy lounging on floor pillows by the crackling fire. But, likely, the window seat attracts more attention especially at sunset when the rugged landscape blazes with color.

Opposite: *Antique trunks with iron handles serve as both end tables and hideaways for books and magazines. Pulling the chairs and furniture away from the wall and allowing them to float makes better use of the space and also stretches the room visually.*

Architect: Bennett Wagner Grody; Designer: In-site Design Group

With no alteration in colors and no jarring surface treatments, the designer carves separate zones for living. The pale, silky smooth wood floor flows from sitting area to dining area, but the ceiling changes: A low soffit near the gleaming dining table beams above the table and chairs. An interesting arrangement of cabinetry blocks the dining table from the living room while allowing traffic to flow freely on both sides. The owners could use the wall-to-ceiling cabinet to store their china, silver, and linens. The waist-high segment of cabinetry performs as a serving station and buffet. And while this cabinetry wall is straight-edged, a bar area on the other side of the dining room entrance is curved to be user-friendly to all. There's a plentiful supply of art, but the living room steals the winning focal point in the floor-to-ceiling glass doors and all that lies beyond.

Left: *Shine and sparkle add to the feeling of spaciousness, from the glass shelving in cabinets to the chrome-framed dining chairs. Glass and bright metal are repeated again in the hanging lamp suspended above the table.*

Right: *One piece of spectacular art is often more effective than a variety. And accents of black add punch. To soften the room's formality, a catchy mismatched chair has been moved in.*

Designer: Eric Mitchell Shore Design; Manufacturer: Charlie Hallam

Forms that are reminiscent of those popular in the 1950s play an important role in this very understated room—from the sensuously curved sofas to the striking sculpture suspended above the hearth. There's a definite rhythm and flow, and it gives the space energy. Such fluidity means bright colors and accessories are unnecessary. The collection of warm cream and earthy brown tones seems to collect the sun and heat the space naturally, instead. Keeping the palette simple in a room with plenty of glass also places nature on center stage. The windows that lead to the blue ocean and the green trees link the indoor setting to its glorious outdoor site. The light-toned floor appears to mesh with the adjoining deck, too, which gives the streamlined room the aura of additional space. To duplicate this style, look for quality reproductions with similar tailored silhouettes and include an ottoman.

Right: *Circular motion also translates a round wood seat, which functions at times as a handy extra table, and a small gold sculpture, which appears to be whirling above the fireplace. The two vases guarding the hearth's opening add some balance to the design while adhering to the color scheme.*

Opposite: *A simple shift in glass from clear to frosted interjects a note of mystery. On one side of the fireplace, the view is clear sky and trees; on the other, it's more like an Asian garden. Leaves are revealed, but the smoky glass hides neighboring houses and keeps the room private.*

Left: *A large mirror atop the mantel gathers extra light and makes the room seem airier. Light-collecting white tiles on the hearth act much the same way. Well-lit oil paintings are traditional fare, but notice how the modern artwork by the lamp is also included to keep the room up to date and fresh.*

An assembly of soft upholstered furniture entices family and friends to stay and make themselves at home in this cheerful living room. As cozy as an English cottage, the space also includes smaller armchairs that can be moved into place for a crowd and plenty of tables for setting down a cup of tea or a wine glass. The color scheme is simple but effective: a white backdrop, an assortment of rosy hues and patterns, and for elegance, jolts of jet-black. Decorative objects, oil paintings, silver, and piles of art books help build a mood that is as traditional as plum pudding but also very inviting. Formal but not stuffy, the cozy room gains extra character with sumptuous window treatments and an Oriental carpet. The skillful combination of materials, such as the glass coffee table, the bamboo side table, and the wood barrel, adds a merry edge to the pleasing refinement.

Above: *The cushy furnishings show off decorative piping that complements the pinks and greens of the draperies. Comfort also results in plenty of plump pillows for leaning back and a classic seating arrangement that encourages hours of leisurely conversation.*

For a unique living or family room, look to unusual furnishings that are equally as comfortable as they are original. For instance, a charming iron-framed chaise in this spacious setting has taken over the best view in the house, claiming the large arched window as its partner. Just like a love seat or a sofa, the chaise provides a nest for afternoon daydreaming as well as nighttime reading. Coupled with a modernist iron standing lamp (on the left) and a wisp of a sheltering curtain, it's become a perfect place for relaxation. The wood floor and glass table are interesting clean-lined foils for the space's more elaborate elements like the draped round table, the decorative folding screen, and the traditional fringed sofa. Recruit some healthy green plants, particularly ones that can be suspended from the ceiling, and you can conjure up a similar conservatorylike ambience without compromising the modernistic approach with lots of unwieldy flowerpots and boxes.

Right: *The theatrical chord that sweeps back the gossamer drape, the iron candle-holder, and the decorative box are planned to catch the eye with their diverse tactile qualities. The soft throw and pillows are set cued to increase comfort.*

Left: *Notice how the decorative screen and rug share similar colors. The distressed sideboard (in the forefront) is linked in color to the sofa and the pale chaise covering. The iron sidechairs are a good match to the whimsical birdcage, while twin palms and other plants add green to lessen the room's starkness.*

Designer: Adrienne Rich

Left: *From the kitchen, the cook looks out on an inviting scene including a roaring fire. Decoration in the great room is kept to a minimum. Stone crocks, a painted tray table, and highly collectible, round Shaker wood baskets make a fine hideaway for doo-dads as well as necessities like tea bags and matches.* Above: *Arranged in an L-shape, the two sofas delineate a pleasant area for conversation and television-watching. The rustic beams overhead help create a cozy mood that, with so much glass, is never dreary. Instead, morning and afternoon light enrich the scene's carefully monitored antiquity.*

Long ago, the earliest American settlers made do with one or two multipurpose rooms. It wasn't until the Colonists began to prosper that the idea of adding rooms for specific purposes like sleeping and eating came to be. This versatile great room with its picturesque beamed ceiling and classic white walls and blue-green trim combination accommodates any number of activities including relaxing and dining. And, to assure the setting remains filled with light at all times, an entire wall has been turned over to windows. Two sofas interject color with their bright contemporary pumpkin-orange upholstery, too. However, in character with the architecture, traditional-style cabinetry hides modern conveniences like the television. And a friendly mix of collectibles takes advantage of the room's higher reaches. Inside the antique blanket chest that serves as a coffee table, games and books can be stored to keep small children as happy as the adults.

A timeless, elegant air envelops this formal living space. Calling on tradition, the walls are painted a classic lemony hue, a crystal-bedecked chandelier fathers the dainty sconces over the mantel, and table lamps are discreetly placed to yield pools of warm light just where they are most needed. A studied symmetry in objects and furnishings (anchored at one end of the room with the fireplace and at the other by a large window) measure up to the room's handsome architectural details. The lovely floor-to-ceiling fringed valances and drapes—pulled back to let in the light—add grace. No doubt about it, this is a room designed to be enjoyed primarily by grown-ups. The two conversation areas make the well-proportioned space suitable for large gatherings as well as intimate groups. And a grand piano—always a luxury object—delivers music for all occasions.

Above: *A sisal carpet is overlaid with a needlepoint rug to add richness and pump up the comfort quotient. Deep fringe on the sofa also brings a note of luxury to the scene. The needlepoint dog pillow and the black-and-white family photographs are cozy touches in an otherwise dressy room.*

Opposite: *A crisp white ceiling and white trim are the right contrasts for the pale yellow walls. A gold mirror like the one here above the mantel and shiny brass andirons in front of the fireplace are appropriate for such a setting, too. The curved-back love seat nicely balances the twin armchairs across the way.*

Everything about this arresting living room is opulent and totally original. Note how traditional moldings look down on a modern honey-toned wood wall complete with a fireplacelike sculpture. The fluid forms of the furnishings and the glass tables speak of the '50s. But the architecture seems more old world. A standard sofa, of course, would have looked too ordinary for a room that wears drapes emblazoned with shiny scraps of mirror. Instead, a two-sided chaise with an array of pillows was chosen. In addition to providing a place for sitting and conversing, the upholstered chaise delivers a bit of Los Angeles-screen-star magic to the setting. Small accessories play a bit part too. Pieces of art glass and miniature vases filled with fresh flowers interject a friendly human touch. Even though this room may be lavish in its presentation, it is also welcoming.

Right: *You're not exactly snuggling up to a fire here, but the warm hue of the wood and the subtle jolts of vibrant color make it just as inviting. Devise a similar scheme for your home by mixing curvy '50s furniture with current pieces.*

Designer: Christopher Coleman

Opposite: *Keeping pace with the rest of the scene, a glowing boxlike chandelier lights the chaise. The interesting layering effect of old and new along with a contemporary color scheme renders the room ageless.*

Avid readers wanted the congeniality of a multipurpose room where they could cook and dine as well as hunker down with a favorite tome in front of the fire. Casual by nature, these bookworms also envisioned a straightforward room with accessories and art scaled back to a minimum. Luckily, the contemporary architecture of their home lends itself perfectly to a flexible floor plan with a utilitarianlike hearth. On one side of the fireplace lies the dining area, and on the other is the inviting sitting room with a comfortable couch and a large coffee table for unfolding papers or comparing notes. Books have found a neat home in floor-to-ceiling shelves that also could incorporate the sound system. Track lighting pinpoints the best-sellers, while the concrete floor and birch veneer cabinetry keep the scene looking light and airy. All in all, it's a story with a happy ending.

Right: Birch cabinets—some open, some closed—tie the dining area and the sitting room together. The cement floor also helps unify the spaces. Having decided on a modern hearth, the homeowners use the flat top to display seasonal gatherings or favorite collectibles.

Right: A dark coffee table would have made the small sitting area feel cramped. Glass lends the same amount of workable space without making the room seem tighter. The low wall between the hearth and the cabinets could be put to use as a staging area or bar.

Architects: Burt & Weinrich Architects

Scrumptious peach-colored walls, set off with a white ceiling and white crown molding, make this English-flavored living room pleasingly cocoonlike. The Oriental carpet, the matching upholstery, and the abundance of art could have added up to a very formal scene. But a cache of subtle touches—the mantel decoration, the mismatched stands flanking the hearth, the sofa's flouncy skirt, and the paisley shawl so casually tossed—loosen the restraints. Thoughtful gestures like plenty of pillows for relaxing in comfort and a bowl of help-yourself fruit bear a distinct message of welcome. Even an identical pair of elegant topiaries doesn't lessen the snug, let's-sit-awhile-and-talk air. In winter when the fire is lit or in summer when guests are invited to share a glass of lemonade, this well-put-together room is a welcoming backdrop. Visitors perceive it as a haven that has lovingly evolved over time. What could be nicer than that?

Left: *The coffee table with its Chippendale-style handles and its handy drawer is a good weight for the bulky pieces that surround it. At a comfortable height, the table can accommodate the needs of several people.*

Above: *A sturdy ottoman affords extra flexibility serving as a seat or serving table. Swept back to show the garden, the chintz drapes are gracious but, minus a lavish valance and trim, not overly formal. The heart motif, which appears on the pine stand, is an age-old decorative theme.*

Editing furnishings and letting in the sun are two popular decorating strategies. They are an unbeatable double punch that results in rooms that are inviting, comfortable, and filled with the tenor of a new millennium. Add to this a palette of serene colors such as icy blue and barely warm yellow, and the scene just gets better. Airy spaces like this one can't help but elevate your mood. Deftly arranged to maximize the amount of available square footage, the living room features not one but two generous sitting areas. And where the one has the outdoors as a focal point, the other centers itself on a large contemporary painting. Where the sun is most evident, the furnishings are snowy white; move in toward the core of the house, though, and they are dark leather and chrome. The pale floor distributes light to both. No matter where you land, the fantastic, uplifting ambience prevails.

Left: *Interesting architecture like this demands a decoration that enhances the shape and form of each room. With this in mind, furnishings are kept low so as not to detract from the view and floors are swept clean. The curved cabinet filled with books deftly guards the window-side conversation area.*

Right: *Repeating colors tie the main living spaces together. Note how the contemporary rug displays bolts of blue similar to the blue of the vases and other decorative objects scattered throughout the first floor. In a large space, small details garner a great deal of attention.*

The guidelines for creating a comfortable family space have been followed to a tee: unifying colors, plenty of lighting for reading as well as mood setting, and an entire wall of windows to let in the sun. Once whitewashed, this not-overly grand-size room appeared to open up. The pristine beams, ceiling, and paneling are a complementary background for an interesting array of materials: woven and iron chairs, wicker baskets, and assorted antiques. Every seat can access a convenient space to set down a drink or book, too. And there's a strong sense of personal style that washes over everything: the touches of green ivy, for example, both real and faux that spring up at either end of the room and the family photographs. No one who enters here will be in any hurry to leave soon and that, from conception to creation, was the whole idea.

Above: *Nubby uphol-stery in a comforting wheat color is a good partner to the pat-terned fabric that appears on the major-ity of seat cushions. Teamed with green plants and a variety of wood tones, including this rough-legged stool, the mix of textures brews a fresh, outdoorsy atmosphere.*

Right: *Two tiers of drapes are a bit of sumptuousness in an otherwise casual room. Drapes on the iron rod are most often called into service, but having an additional layer ratchets up the luxury factor. Chandeliers poke light into the ceiling's farthest corners, which renders the room cozier at night.*

Designer: Mark Polo/Polo, M.A. Interior Design

Island Paradise

A riot of upbeat color, a wealth of textures, and a splash of whimsy give this globally inspired room a personality all its own. Moroccan- and Indian-like fabrics light up the subdued background walls and ceilings like fireworks. Sensational colors such as hot red, orange, and yellow never go unnoticed, but set against the green-gray walls, they ignite a volcano of interest. To keep the tropical living-is-easy beat pumping, the couches are low (better for lounging) and swamped with pillows. And the chairs are lightweight, natural-colored wicker. With a minimum of effort, such seats can be moved around to accommodate a number of people. Grab a pillow, in fact, and you can make yourself very comfortable on top of one of the kilim rugs. Of course, an island in the South Seas has flowers so this one does as well, and they're fiery blossoms that interject more perfume and color into this paradise's air.

Opposite: *Simple shades at the window keep the attention focused on the furnishings and the fabrics. To amplify the ambience, the lighting includes a pierced shade (on the standing lamp) and a bounty of candles. The frog sculpture is a humorous conversation piece beloved by all.*

Right: *Work and travel were the inspirations for this rich palette. The tableaux of patterns is made more successful because of the backdrop. Short on color but long on texture, the walls are reminiscent of bark, the sort you could find in a tropical beach hut.*

Meals aside, a kitchen is also a place where memories are made. Eyeing a child's first drawing, opening a perfect report card, or making an engagement announcement often occur to the tune of a whistling kettle. It's not surprising that a workable, pleasing kitchen is one of a home's top-selling attractions and a pleasure for all who frequent it.

To accommodate the ebb and flow of family and friends, a good layout is essential. While you might like having company, you don't want them underfoot. Instead, there should be well-defined traffic routes and a zone where the chef functions undisturbed. How many people cook at one time (experts advise 48 to 54 inches of space for one person to pass safely behind another), children's ages, and any special needs family members have should all be taken into consideration.

There are four basic kitchen layouts: the galley shape with two walls of appliances squaring off opposite each other; the L-shape that locates the three main elements (sink, stove, and refrigerator) along two perpendicular walls forming a natural triangle; the U-shape that puts the elements on three walls; and the Gshape, which is essentially a U-shape with a fourth wall (which could be a handy peninsula) to provide room for more counter space, cabinetry, and appliances. For efficiency, consider the classic work triangle formula according to how it coincides with the configuration you choose. Two work areas—one for cooking, the other for serving and clearing, each with a sink—is also a popular strategy.

As an alternative to costly remodeling, how about changing the color and finish of cabinets, counters, flooring, and walls? Wood cabinets, for instance, can be sanded and repainted in a current color like khaki. A laminate counter and backsplash could be updated with creamy limestone.

Modern kitchens maintain their clean look by providing a niche for every element. Cabinet manufacturers feature hundreds of options including clever interior fittings for silverware, appliance garages (great for taking advantage of deep corners), and custom panels for disguising appliances. In general, cherry- or mahogany-paneled and glass-front doors afford traditional appeal. Blonde wood, laminate, metal, and new options like mesh inset panels are typical of contemporary rooms. Oak or maple raised panel doors that are painted or stained say country.

Be ingenious about finding extra inches. Attempt to have 12 inches of landing space on either side of any cooking surface as a safety feature. If there's no room for an island, what about extending the counter to accommodate stools? Will a built-in folding table that extends when you need it and drops down when you don't provide a roost? Also, consider pullout work surfaces for various chores.

A breakfast nook—two parallel benches with the table between or benches perpendicular to one another with the table spanning the open side—takes up less space than a table with chairs. The convenient-height benches are easily accessible for wheelchair users and safer for little kids than stools. Cozy banquettes (with seats 15 inches deep or more) are well suited for a country/cottage or retro kitchen. Use a playful color combination like yellow, red, and white for the upholstery. Or select another hue from the swinging '40s and

'50s such as gold, turquoise, lavender (for a new twist try pairing lavender with celadon or sage), or light green.

Extend a row of cabinets into the breakfast area to visually link the areas and to gain storage. Repeating a surface, laminate on the countertops and the tabletop in the bay lends cohesion, so will echoing tile or wallpaper colors in cushions and curtains. Forego upper cabinets to render a cramped kitchen more open. Glass-door cabinets—like all gleaming surfaces—help bounce light around and keep a kitchen looking sunrise-fresh. To capture light from an adjoining dining room or enclosed porch, install French doors. And consider knocking down the wall to a room that's rarely used to create a convenient pantry.

White appliances continue to rule, but black and stainless steel are close behind. Many homeowners opt to blend refrigerators and dishwashers with cabinetry, but appliances can also be used to garner attention. A commercial-style stainless-steel refrigerator takes on a sculptural quality in a sun-washed modern kitchen.

Old or vintage-looking furniture exudes charm. For a delightful eclectic demeanor, scoot in a hutch to hold Mexican pottery in the breakfast room. Repeat the classic bright yellow and cobalt blue colors in a valance and tie-on seat pads. Or juxtapose a Shaker-style bench with a banquette. A farm table could be a workstation for mixing salads or making sandwiches in a room sans an island.

Give the kitchen your personal stamp by incorporating favorite collectibles.

It's hard to pinpoint what you notice first: the enticing, saturated citrus color of the walls and ceiling, the rocketlike exhaust hood hovering above the shiny cooktop, or the subtle cohesion of appliances and cabinetry. A full sweep of solid surface countertop and Euro-style streamlined cabinets—in a delicious shade of gray-green—cook up a pared-down, inviting kitchen that functions every bit as well as it looks. Should the cooks require a pot or a pan, they need only reach into one of the deep pullout drawers. Every spice bottle, every dish, and every cup has its place, and this translates not only efficiency, but a very clean and organized look for a busy person who also likes to cook. No other embellishments are necessary except lots of natural light and a little time; this minimalist kitchen is a simply inspiring place to prepare a favorite menu for others.

Above: *The height of the cabinets is at a perfect level for displaying a vase of flowers as well as items you don't need to call into service every day. Below, a wider than usual toe kick lends the design stability.*

Right: *Thin, angular metal handles define the shape of the cabinet doors. On the cabinet beneath the sink, the handle is run up and down to visually lengthen the door and the corner area.*

Opposite: *A glass-block window is very much in keeping with the room's contemporary tenor. It brings in the light, without yielding any privacy. Frosted-glass cabinet inserts blur what's behind so there's no worry if the contents—one day—are a little less than neat.*

Everything is more in this stately room, and that's the appeal. The high-arched ceiling makes way for three tiers of traditionally styled white cabinets, an extra-large freezer/refrigerator, and a soapstone sink with not one but a trio of faucets! The vast amount of space provides extra inches—make that feet—for a handsome dining table and chairs as well as a sun-yellow enameled range. The large chandelier above the table, in fact, is a congenial companion to the oversize steel range hood. Guests can hunker down in the kitchen, and there's still plenty of room for a cook to perform.

Below: *A pair of dishwashers and a wine fridge are just two of the luxurious extras in a kitchen fit for royalty. Soft seats on the otherwise prim and proper dining chairs ensure family and friends sit comfortably.*

Everywhere you look there is storage—glass-front cabinets, pullout drawers upon drawers, and open shelves—to lend a wee bit of homeyness. If you don't have the square footage to duplicate this room, copy the look with white cabinets and stainless-steel appliances. If possible, move in a table and a pretty chandelier. The end result may not be quite as flamboyant, but everyone's home is a castle.

Opposite: *With a table for guests handy, the cook need not feel deprived of company. Granite countertops and two refrigerators maintain restaurant-quality efficiency in the major work zone.*

Architect: Doug McIntosh; Designer: Pamela Bytner, CKD; Manufacturer: Craft-Maid Kitchens

Who said old and new can't mix? Take the best of what you love from the past and partner it with all of today's amenities for a kitchen that will be the envy of the neighborhood. That's exactly what happened in this attractive New Mexico kitchen. The painted white cabinets, the stainless-steel countertops, and the geometric range hood place the room squarely in the 21st century. But the charming island—a look-alike for an antique farmhouse table—defies the too-new label. So do the bin pulls and the stretch of low-key wood counter that surrounds the auxiliary sink. The warm brick floor and the ceiling beams are traditional, but the mood is definitely not your elder's kitchen with ruffled curtains and pot holders. In step with the times, this room assigns each piece of equipment its own resting spot and affords the chef room to work. It's an all-business attitude with a touch of nostalgia, and it will feel just right if you're straddling the divide between classic and contemporary.

Left: *The dark-stained farmhouse table may exude old-fashioned appeal, but it's a modern-day work-horse. The flat panel drawer fronts conceal storage for everyday necessities. The stainless-steel feet give it an extra kick of up-to-date personality.*

Right: *Two floating shelves in lieu of upper cabinets are modern choices for storage. Glasses are there when you need them. The smaller sink is a perfect bar sink for entertaining.*

Designer: Joan Viele, CKD; Manufacturer: Dura Supreme

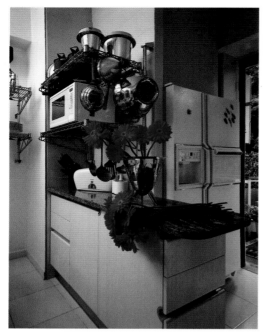

Throwing standard formulas to the wind, this kitchen was designed to be tidy and practical. With that in mind, utilitarian steel shelving is combined with contemporary flat-front cabinetry. The steel shelves house the microwave, extra dishes, and less frequently used pieces while the cabinets keep everyday necessities and food supplies close at hand. With counter space provided on both sides of the narrow room, the cook has a choice of where to work. Or two people—despite the kitchen's diminutive size—can work smoothly together. Instead of matching appliance models, the owners chose items based on the room's palette of white, cream, and gray. Even though the varying colored items may seem to be sporadically placed in order to tie the room together with color, they are put in positions of convenience. For instance, the refrigerator sits contentedly across from the stainless-steel range, with the sink close by. A small dining table and chairs provide a stopover for meals. Or—weather permitting—you can easily grab a plate of food and head outside to dine alfresco.

Above: *Stainless-steel storage units such as these are convenient and easy to install. Such shelving is also a proven method for keeping a kitchen looking open. The granite counter is good for salad-fixing and dough-rolling.*

Architect: Angelo Luigi Tartaglia

Left: *A single painting sets the owners' choice of neutral colors in motion. To make use of every bit of storage, cookbooks are filed on top of the cabinets for quick reference. Below, stainless steel makes a germ-resistant, long-wearing, and light-reflective backsplash.* Right: *The granite tabletop matches the counters. When the cook requires more room for a project such as making jam or holiday cookie-decorating, the durable table can be used as a work surface.*

Frontier Land

Rustic log homes go to great lengths to re-create the look and feel of the past. Modern conveniences are usually hidden or disguised so as not to intrude upon the recreation of pioneer spirit. This modest, but personality-packed breakfast room is a perfect example. Country memorabilia teamed with simple furnishings help fashion a charming setting that is suited to the rest of the house but also just right for an early-morning wake-up call. The barn-red trim around the windows and the red of the wall cupboard and cabinet pull our attention away from the handy sink that's tucked into a corner. In early American houses, similar cupboards were used to store china, glass, and cutlery, and they were almost always painted. Picking up on the theme, red-and-white-checked curtains add another dollop of cheerfulness. And everywhere the eye rests, it sees something interesting.

Right: *Rugged timber walls set the tone for the cozy room. In keeping with their frontier persona, the 19th-century country chairs that were previously painted have been refinished to show off their grain. Checked curtains, like the kind the country's founding members knew, add color.*

Left: *Wide-plank floors and a wood ceiling complement the architecture and also make the breakfast room seem snug and welcoming. Crocheted lace along the open shelves is a dash of romance for a cupboard where collectibles and everyday supplies mingle happily together.*

Above: *Plenty of stone countertop on either side of the range provides the cook with ample work space even when the kitchen is filled with people. Honey-colored cabinets and a pale-tiled floor brighten the scene. Strategically located track lighting also adds to the room's new appeal.* Left: *The symmetrical arrangement of rippled-glass-front cabinets on either side of the range escalates the tidy ambience. Move the plants off the cart when guests arrive, and roll it out for table-side serving.*

Designer: Mark Newman

The bones of this California kitchen were fine. A functional layout was also in place. But what was missing was personality. Today, remodeled with simple wood cabinets and new stainless-steel appliances, the light-washed room has a fresh-as-a-daisy aura. The professional range brings it up to speed in the cooking department, and the cabinetry imbues it with a shipshape tone. However, what really sets it apart is the stainless-steel-top dining table, which will seat a dozen guests. Since the owners favor a casual lifestyle, their best dinner parties transpire in the kitchen. Light-toned chairs with comfortable seats keep the setting looking open. When a group is expected, more chairs are easily added. Aiming for a modern look, decoration is minimal. A wall clock fills the gap above the range perfectly, its round shape being an excellent foil for the boxy cabinets on either side. Time flies, it seems, in this kitchen.

Enlarged by six welcome feet, this kitchen was given a new identity. With wooden beams overhead, the room was already on its way to being warm and welcoming. This newly decorated kitchen has become a colorful, engaging place that wakes the family every morning. Maintaining the essence of a modern New Mexico home, vibrant colors—cobalt blue, turquoise, red, purple, and cantaloupe—were chosen. Against stainless-steel appliances, such retro choices make for a very special—and definitely not boring—kitchen. Right in the middle, a generous-size island holds sway with its confetti-sprinkled top, affording a place for grabbing a bite or just hanging out. Storage, situated around the room, helps the setting stay orderly. But, it's the wonderful color that makes the room so charismatic and endearing to visitors, enticing them to stay.

Above: *Above the sink, the jazzy cantaloupe cabinets were fitted with finger pulls rather than hardware to give them a lighter look. Extra-thick edges along the speckled countertops lend visual weight to make the island seem more substantial.*

Right: *White counter-tops include confetti-like sprinkles of color similar to those on the cabinets. The red counter nestled beside the oven is a whimsical touch designating "hot," a good visual reminder for house-holds with kids. Glass inserts alter the look of the turquoise cabinets by the windows.*

Opposite: *Cheerful accents of color dropped in the tile floor keep everybody's feet tapping. The wide island offers lots of storage and provides enough room for a sink and a cooktop. For added interest, the brushed chrome cabinet handles vary in size.*

Designer: Joan Viele, CKD; Manufacturer: Neff Cabinets

Above: *Convenient features in this cabinetry include a plate rack, spice drawers, and a nook for a wine rack. Task lighting beneath the upper cabinets chases away shadows making chores easier.*

Shaker-like knotty pine cabinetry with dark molding helps build a home-sweet-home feeling for the kitchen of a spacious house with barnlike proportions. Combined with a wood ceiling overhead and a wood floor, the pine doors and simple black wrought-iron pulls and knobs foster updated traditional country charm without being overly cute. The gleaming commercial-style stove is highlighted with a backsplash of earthy-hued, oversize tiles and a set of glass-front cabinets. But the other appliances, like the refrigerator, are tucked behind matching panels. Enhancing the kitchen's pull-up-a-stool appeal is the well-planned island that elbows around the work zone without stopping traffic at either end. To avoid monotony, the counter's front is wainscoted and painted green to match the cabinet trim. Another thoughtful idea? The counter's raised height concealing a lower counter and sink where dirty dishes might end up.

Left: *The unadorned wood stove hood is effective in its simplicity. Watching how light plays over the wood's grain and all the knots is part of the beauty of a wood kitchen.*

Right: *One of today's handiest kitchen features—a desk area—uses the same knotty pine cabinetry and wrought-iron hardware as the rest of the space. The handsome dining table and chairs are for more formal dinners.*

Designer: Mary Wisman; Manufacturer: Priemia Cabinets

Above: A round table gobbles up less room in a sunlit spot by the door. Placing the diners where they see the garden is another way to build ambience. With a white cloth and fresh flowers, the enchantment is complete. The painted wall squares are neither old nor new—just fun!

Clearly caught between a love for the old and a hankering for the new? Why sacrifice one style for another? Follow the delightful path illustrated here, and combine the best elements of each. For instance, a gleaming professional-style range can elbow up to plain cabinets and white brick tile and look very much at home. The wood floor helps tie it all together in a warm and friendly manner. Should the shelves vary—some open traditional wood types to hold glass and china, and a wall-mounted steel model stacked with dishes and condiments—it will look charming not out of whack. The deep laundry sink has a European swagger to it that complements this eclectic approach. And a round dining table is both cozy and convenient. Finish off with a bit of a surprise—maybe with a painted checkerboard wall pattern that defies categorization—and the result will be picture-perfect.

Left: *Distressed legs—salvaged from an earlier piece—make great supports for a granite-topped breakfast bar. The black stools are a jolt of elegance and fitting for a room that has glass doorknobs and wood beams! Except for the range, the white appliances fade into the cabinetry making the kitchen airier.* Right: *Modern lighting and old-time bin pulls? Fantastic! The predominance of white prevents the room from seeming the least bit jumbled in time. Instead, classic white tiles and a wood floor welcome the mix-and-match approach.*

With the rough-hewn timbers and plaster ceiling above, you'd know you were in the Southwest. But, no doubt about it, strong Arts and Crafts undertones are also present in this sunny kitchen located in Sante Fe, New Mexico. The room is simple and unadorned so the artisanship and the elements can stand out. At the very heart of the design, the two-level island forges a sitting spot as well as work space. The microwave slips in here at a level for the kids to make a snack. And the granite top and auxiliary sink are an everyday boon for prepping and cooking. But it's the slender furniture-style legs that rocket the island out of the ordinary. Painted deep rich green, the legs complement the tall green hutch that guards the door. Adding the hutch tones down the modernity of the hard-edged granite and stainless steel. The natural red birch floor is a peacemaker, pulling the factors congenially together.

Right: *At the raised butcher-block end of the island, the cook can sit and scan a cookbook. The island's lower end features a granite top. Open storage is beneficial for large mixing bowls and baskets. Across the room, the pass-through leads to a formal dining room.*

Opposite: *The full-height granite back-splash is striking and practical. A series of hidden built-ins, which might feature special units to hold pot lids, cookie sheets, and trays, swallow up all the debris leaving the cooking zone and the kitchen neat as a pin.*

Architect: Turner Lechner & Romero; Designer: Joan Viele, CKD

Left: *A peninsula of cabinets—some high, some low—provides storage and counter space. The upper cabinet's glass doors enhance the kitchen's light.*

Reservations, please! This contemporary kitchen is all shiny surfaces, and they're inviting. Gleaming black counters and unadorned wood are classic partners on a modern menu. Should you crave a room of this caliber, think out of the box. Use curves rather than corners, for instance, at the cabinet's end. Mimic those curves with a weighty round pillar. And, shape your counter into a circle—like the table at your favorite restaurant. Keep in mind, country stools at this dining establishment are not allowed. Instead, search out modern-looking seats, and then go one better and award them plush coverings of color: purple, red, or gold. A glass-block window and vertical blinds on glass doors agree with this sort of elegant Euro look more than curtains or drapes. Pièce de résistance? The stone tile with different colors and gradations gives that extra bit of spice.

Left: *Hardware is all but eliminated in the narrow cooking zone. Shiny stainless-steel wall ovens are one bit of glimmer—and they just happen to be practical, too. Gone undercover, the fridge is well situated between the cooktop and the ovens.*

Designer: Tom Hasenfang/Richard F. Hendrick, CKD; Manufacturer: Heritage Custom Kitchens

Mixed materials—granite countertops, subway tile backsplash, green and white cabinetry—are only part of this kitchen's scrumptious story. An efficient work triangle figures in, of course, and recessed lights as well as handsome pendant lamps light up the scene with style. A mix of hardware for the cabinetry adds panache. But also of note is how the kitchen is connected to the very appealing great room beyond. Family members or guests can grab a plate and help themselves from an island-staged buffet. Then, sail through the expansive arch and claim a seat by the fireplace. Green— the hue of fresh garden vegetables—and accents of sunny yellow bring the spaces comfortably together. A series of open shelves allow the owners to show off their china collection in both rooms. And there are more personal touches like art and flowers to keep the cook happy.

Opposite: *A tongue-and-groove wood ceiling is a fine approach for a traditional-looking kitchen. The footed island also makes the room seem homier as do the substantial stools with their soft tie-on seats. Sheers dressing the glass-front cabinets disguise dishes and food supplies lurking behind.*

Left: *Pretty swags and jabots can be used to dress kitchen windows as long as they are high and out of the way of water and grease. The warm wood floor—sealed for protection—promotes a classic feel that complements simple fixtures and hardware. Throw rugs have nonskid pads for safety.*

Above: *The wood detailing of the mantel complements the style of the cabinets. The pendant lights with stained-glass shades are modern takes on the trendy Tiffany lamps of the late 19th century. At night the colorful glass shades glow like candles above the granite counter.*

Designed to allow enough square footage for some very gracious fireside dining, this appealing barnlike kitchen is well used every day and night. A wood floor and cabinets the color of maple syrup contrast with the white walls and the hefty beams overhead. Sun floods the spacious room through a skylight and unadorned windows by the table. The natural light points out the cabinetry's appealing carvings and moldings as well as the stone tiles unfolding on the cooking zone's walls. This cooking zone is well fitted with places to hide the smaller appliances, deep pullout drawers, and compartmentalized cabinets. The sculptural steel range hood injects some contemporary glitter into the subdued country room. When not in demand, the rattan stools slip under the overhanging granite counter. However, when something is cooking, this trio of stools is considered front row!

Right: *The owners make use of the cabinets' flat top, parking baskets there. Decorative trim and detailing imbues the spacious island with a furniturelike appeal. The bookcase at the island's one end also creates an ideal holding spot for cookbooks and collectibles.*

The Way We Were

Sure, nostalgia has its place. But with today's busy pace, you want a kitchen that also functions up to speed. With a sea of easy-to-clean white brick tiles and a skirted island that has its own make-a-salad or fix-a-drink sink, this could be the one! A quiet beige and white theme harks back to a simpler time. The deep farmhouse sink is up to almost any chore you hand it—even the complex ones. And the restored cooking range may look old but be assured it performs like a pro. Arranged in its own arched alcove—accompanied by a small adjunct table with a butcher-block top—the range is the focal point of the room. The range's chrome accents also tie in beautifully with the stainless-steel fridge. And while the cook wields the pots and pans, guests can assemble on the cozy, comfy banquette. The large square table easily accommodates a hungry crowd.

Right: *The walls of the breakfast room are upholstered. The crisscross ribbons hold an ever-changing roster of family photographs to provoke lively conversation around the table. Two square ottomans on wheels roll up next to the banquette when extra seats are required. The simple hanging lamp is just right for a candle.*

Designer: Mark Cutler Design, Inc.

Right: *The island's sink resembles an antique bowl. White brick tiles—easy to clean and long-lasting—are classic fixtures in vintage kitchens. And look carefully: The skirt beneath the farmhouse sink is lined with the same fabric that graces the window.*

Why leave home when your very own kitchen is as inviting as a country inn? The wood ceiling with its chunky beams and the brick-walled cooking area foster an inviting country mood. The feel is made modern with the addition of light-gathering French doors, stainless-steel appliances, and cabinetry that combines open and closed storage. Wainscoting also helps furnish an old-fashioned but polished finish along the island's front and as a backsplash above the counters. The island is straightforward and, although it guards the cook's busy work zone, is amenable to friends. An iron pot rack makes pots and pans easily available, and earthy-toned canisters hold baking supplies. But, the room veers away from clutter. What's on view—such as the dried flowers and cookbooks—is arranged in a neat fashion, which also helps to promote a more modern persona.

Opposite: *The timber construction is the basis for a rustic mood. A tile floor is used to define the kitchen area from the great room. Materials—red brick, black iron, straw seats on the wood stools—all help prepare a comfortable country mood that spells h-o-m-e.*

Left: *Bountiful storage includes a generous desk area with built-in nooks for letters and bills and cabinetry around the fridge, which includes drawers. The island is long enough for the kids to lay out an after-school project or for five adults to cozy up and not feel crowded.*

Architect/Builder: Mark Wray

Left: *In close proximity to the table, the well-lit counter to the right is used as a serving station and bar. A second sink located here prevents family and friends from lining up at the main sink across the way. Remember: Deep windowsills can hold herb pots!*

Any top chef would warm to this light-filled, efficient room. White cabinetry and brick tile enhance a clean, open feel conducive to cooking. With an abundance of counters and a large sturdy table that can perform as a work surface or even a dining spot, it's easy to prepare an intimate dinner or a celebratory feast for friends. Stainless-steel cabinets on both sides of the businesslike range are stocked with the chef's favorite spices and oils so he can quickly grab what he needs without moving from his command position. A pot spigot is ideal for filling pasta pots right at the range—thus saving more steps. Traditional cabinets surround the room on three sides and feature a variety of storage options. Despite its grand size, the room remains organized. Simple hardware and a wood floor are two more well-thought-out decisions contributing to the kitchen's timeless appeal.

Right: *Maximizing the efficiency of the cooking zone, cabinetry is set above the counters and includes a niche for the microwave as well as appliance garages where smaller tools are stored. The deep drawers could slide out with a slight tug to reveal pots, pans, and lids. Smaller drawers could hold cooking utensils.*

Designer: John and Melia Strittmatter; Manufacturer: Strittmatter Private Label

French country style derives a lot of its flair from the outdoors—blue skies and bright yellow sunflowers. That's the sweet aura that envelops this enchanting kitchen. True to the French penchant for tiles, several tile varieties can be found around the room, providing a number of different functions. Of course, the most eye-catching are the pretty fruit tiles that look as though they're plucked straight from the tree. The scheme of creamy white and pale lemon infuses the room with warmth. For continuity, the range hood is sheathed to match the cabinetry. In fact, so pretty is the overall decoration with the glass-front cabinets and the chandelier, you hardly notice how also very functional this kitchen is. The generous marble-topped island—a treasure for a cook who loves to bake—is fitted with ample storage, including drawers and cupboards, on both sides. And look at the amount of counter!

Below Left: *Accessories and collections play an important role in French country decor. Choose a color—like the buttery yellow associated with Provence shown here—and begin accumulating your own hoard of beautiful plates and teapots. The light-colored wood plate rack also fits the look.* Below Right: *A six-burner cooktop translates some heavy-duty cooking. And a backsplash of good-enough-to-eat, hand-painted fruit tiles provides charm. For practicality, storage and counters surround the chef on all sides. Simple hardware allows the more dramatic features to dominate.*

French rooms often mix neutrals and creams, or creams with swaths of Mediterranean color. Using the color red (another favorite hue from Provence) as an accent, bring in red-and-white-checked dish towels and a bunch of fresh flowers. A wood floor will show off your color scheme to best advantage.

Dedicated collectors of American 18th- and 19th-century antiques often don't want a modern-looking kitchen. In love with the past, they envision the same sort of layout that our ancestors had. Long ago, the kitchen was often a fireplace located in what was then labeled the "keeping room." This intriguing kitchen in a Colonial-style home takes its cue from that history. Appliances are revealed, but the traditional cabinetry and the butcher-block counters give the room the right sort of early-American flavor. Distressed to look authentic, the painted cabinets even sport artificial wear marks in all the right places. A tall wooden board on the counters keeps dirty dishes hidden from sight; while overhead a galaxy of old wicker baskets and well-used copper pots and pans add to the period character. In the end, it's the best of both worlds: a practical kitchen that maintains the home's integrity.

Left: *A historic paint color in a matte finish is ideal for cabinetry and trim, and it is a smart contrast to the white walls and ceiling. For such a decor, smooth pine makes the most authentic-looking floor in the dining area; where traffic is heaviest, brick is a fitting substitute.* Above: *On summer days, French doors are flung open to connect the unfussy, brick-floored kitchen to a brick courtyard. The soft blue and white tile backsplash helps to define the cooking area. The crock that holds utensils and the folksy baskets are gestures the Colonists would have appreciated.*

Some kitchens—and this is one—have "home" written all over them. As cheerful as a cookie jar, this room evokes an upbeat, sunny mood with just a few splashes of bright color and a whole lot of traditional cabinetry. Most of the appliances stay hidden behind matching panels, giving the space a more finished, clean-lined look. Still, from the vibrant-colored pottery on the open shelves to the fabrics, this is a place geared for nurturing: It has good food, a comfy window seat, and interesting nooks and corners, like a mini-breakfast bar for snacks. Adjoining an elegant great room with a fireplace, the kitchen maintains a more simple, down-to-earth demeanor. The wood floor may connect the two spaces, but their personalities are vastly different. Think cocktails by the handsome hearth and hot chocolate with marshmallows in this totally inviting kitchen.

Above: Planned as an adjunct perch for two, the tiny granite breakfast bar welcomes early-morning or late-night visitors. Beadboard on the island's base complements the cabinets' style. Yellow pillows are additional rays of sunshine.

Right: *Wall ovens—located next to the baking station—take on any number of cooking chores simultaneously. Canisters hold flour and sugar; equipment such as rolling pins and pans are in the cupboard and drawers below. Detailing on the upper cabinets is reminiscent of the Arts and Crafts style.*

Opposite: *Beadboard cabinet fronts and bin pulls help deliver a traditional feel for the spacious room. And they make a great cover for the fridge. Should a child—or mom—want to rest, they can stretch out on the window seat for a few minutes.*

Designer: Louis Nardo-lillo, CKD; Manufacturer: Heritage Custom Kitchens

Blue-as-the-Mediterranean tiles transform a small city kitchen into a larger-than-life superstar! Selecting the same color tiles for walls and floor—and coupling them with a plain white ceiling for contrast—produces a much more dramatic effect than would just one method without the other. Against the heady blue background, the white cabinets and appliances snap to their best attention. The plain-front Euro-style cabinets won't settle for ordinary either, though. Two clear fronts break up the sameness and keep the cabinetry from appearing top-heavy. The little island comes across as dainty (thanks to its pristine white base), but it's also a very accessible work area for the cook. And, off in the corner out of harm's way, there's a quiet location for a good-size breakfast table and four chairs. Cleverly designed soffits focus light on all the right places, too, so no one's ever in the dark.

Right: *Light-collecting glass doors have intriguing accents of blue and yellow to complement the kitchen's blue color scheme, while the black table and chairs echo the tile's dark grout lines. On the cook's side of the island, pullout drawers could contain table utensils and linens.*

Opposite: *A pair of stools and a small granite counter like this are all that's required when you want to share a moment. The counter's overhang would even provide room for a third stool, should you decide to invite a friend. To maintain the unfettered look, a simple white blind dresses the kitchen window.*

Architect: Angelo Luigi Tartaglia

Left: *This up-to-date Shaker-like island replicates an old table right down to its dainty turned legs. Smartly fitted with storage, the island hides modern equipment. Clutter would mar the scene so there are plenty of cabinets wherever they're most needed; for instance, to hold pots and pans next to the industrial range.*

The 17th-century Dutch painter Jan Vermeer is well known for his clean, light-filled interiors. His rooms, like this one, portray a certain stillness that impacts viewers emotionally. A clean-lined farmhouse kitchen of this nature doesn't require an excess of color or an overload of furnishings. The beauty of the room lies in the gracious architecture, particularly the high ceiling, the simple materials, and the soothing palette. The undressed windows usher in sunlight that sweeps across the wood floor, subtly warming the spacious room in a way more exuberant paint colors or fabrics could never do. Still, to afford some visual weight and to help keep the scene balanced, the dining area is set more dramatically. The black spindle-back chairs and the two-toned table are anchored on a cheerful checkerboard rug, a fine foil to the striped rug in the cooking area. Certainly, Vermeer, a stickler for details, would approve.

Right: *The simple stencil that sweeps around the border of the room adds just the slightest hint of color and is appropriate in a kitchen that looks to the past but in a fresh, pared-down manner. The wall-mounted cabinets mimic antique cupboards. And for washing dishes or vegetables, the farmhouse sink is ideal.*

Designer: Kuche
Cucina/Amir Ilin

Prim and Proper

Sometimes a new house can be more of a challenge when it comes to creating a warm country-inspired look. But not so for this kitchen. The honey-toned oak floor warms the welcoming room from the bottom up. And a bumper crop of cabinets—all white as fresh farm eggs—do their part, too. With so many clever hiding spots, including a generous appliance garage, equipment and supplies are kept orderly and out of sight. Bring in a pretty, small-patterned floral paper to play off the golden wood and the spanking white, and you've fashioned a kitchen that everyone will love. Sweet valances and tie-back curtains also ratchet up the homey mood. Best of all, while the cook works, friends and family sitting at the table can keep him company. If they're here at the right time, he may even present them with a fresh-out-of-the-oven apple pie!

Right: *This kitchen employs an efficient U-shape floor plan to save lots of unnecessary steps. The peninsula defines the room's largest chunk of space as the cooking area and works as a serving station for dining. The Mission-style round oak table and chairs complement the floor.*

Left: *Since washing up generates lots of splashing, the window above the sink was dressed with a valance but no curtains. Dainty hand-painted tiles in the backsplash mimic the wallpaper's floral pattern for an extra bit of visual interest. The traditional-style brass hardware is also a stylish touch.*

Designer: Lauren Rosenberg-Moffit/ Rosenberg-Moffit Interior Design

A multicolored collection of vintage dishware and pottery was the kick-off for this happy-go-lucky room. The lovable hues of pitchers, plates, and cups inspired the owners to craft a kitchen as bright as a new penny. Metal cabinets and a checkerboard linoleum floor add in-character vibes as does the scalloped wood valance above the sink. But it's the retro styling that makes you really want to pull up a chair. To enhance the cheerful mood, the tiled backsplash in the cooking zone copycats the color of the collectibles. And even the café curtains dupli-cate a water pitcher's yellow glaze. A simple desk area pro-vides a cook with a place to jot

Above: *The window seat's lift-up top makes it a handy storage vehicle for vintage linens. The miniature desk area is a gift to cook and child alike. While a parent works at the table, a young-ster can perch here and draw. The metal stool is in keeping with the room's easygoing nature.*

down a recipe, and a window seat that's big enough for two invites company. Collec-tors generally like any prop that relates to their favorite treasures so there are vintage fabric on the pillows and a 1940/1950 tablecloth at mealtime.

Left: *Simple open shelves show off the ever-increasing collectibles to their best advantage. Centered in the middle of the sunny room, the table serves dual purposes: food prepara-tion and casual dining. The old kitchen chairs have been revamped with a coat of snappy white paint.*

A small kitchen minus windows could live its whole life in despair. But not this shipshape room. A well-designed lighting scheme more than makes up for the lack of natural light. The red oak plank floor and the maple cabinets also help brighten and warm the space. Teamed with maple butcher-block counters, the overall theme is almost monochromatic, which makes a small kitchen look a bit larger than it really is. In addition to the counters, metal posts and fittings support a peninsula that can serve as either a food preparation site or a party serving station. A standard cabinet in the same spot would have overwhelmed the new design and diminished the forward-thinking look the metal base provides. Final plus? The cook and guests adore the simple but efficient layout. With pedestrian routes planned on both sides of the peninsula, traffic never comes to a standstill.

Right: *In place of the usual pot rack, an iron pipe does the job. A simple exhaust fan—rather than an elaborate hood—also helps the kitchen maintain a more open look. The steel backsplash running along the sink wall catches light and complements the look of the peninsula's metal base.*

Opposite: *Low-key maple cabinets give the cook space for food supplies as well as gear. And counters are located where they are most needed—on either side of the range and beside the sink. The wood floor helps to unite the kitchen to the surrounding rooms.*

Delectable Dining Rooms

There are those who would trade anything to have a separate dining room, others pooh-pooh the one they have as a wasted bit of space and shut the door. The first group has nothing to envy since there are myriad ways to forge comfortable, part-time dining areas in other rooms. The naysayers can take heart, too. With some adjustments, their forlorn rooms can be made as satisfying as mom's home cooking.

Any room with a few square feet to spare such as family rooms and dens—particularly those lined with books or French doors—make spectacular mealtime settings. Position a table to one side of the room, figuring about 8 square feet for a table for 4, plus around 36 inches for the chair pull-out. Or hire a carpenter to build a stationary bench flush against the wall. Place a skinny pine table in front and ladder-back chairs opposite.

Tuck a drop-leaf table that's ready to do double duty in a spacious entry hall. One moment it's a hall table, the next it seats special guests. The round table beside the family room sofa? A romantic oasis. Cover the table with a colored cloth, pull up some seats, and light the fire. Diverse chair styles add drama: wing chairs, love seats, and even ottomans (as long as they roll). Flexible dining should be as easy as pie.

Collect benches that slide or feather-light wicker chairs to nestle up to a salvaged garden table.

Storage? In addition to cabinetry, consider plate racks, wall shelves, and corner china cupboards. All these use little space while providing handy inches.

Reinvent forlorn dining rooms with suitable furnishings, paint, and fabric. The right table—set on a bright area rug or centered on a window—can be your anchor. A round table, the favorite for conversation, softens a boxy room; a small square table does well in tight quarters; long farmhouse-type tables work best in rectangular rooms. And for ambience find a stunning electric or candle-holding chandelier.

Warm colors stimulate conversation. Paint walls a soft red, or cover them with a richly textured or patterned wallcovering. Soft contemporary hues like hydrangea-purple and pistachio-green teamed with crisp white moldings will imbue the room with a Monet-garden air. Slipcover dining chairs, or add simple seat cushions in a contrasting color or a pleasing floral pattern.

Above: *An Oriental rug anchors the comfortable sitting area where guests sojourn for an after-dinner conversation. The gold accent table, at the sofa's end, ties in with the dining chairs as does the white upholstery.*

Why is it when we think of dining rooms we imagine the same old table with the perfunctory chairs? Take notice of this very stylish arrangement for cues on how to fashion your own captivating dining area. Standing just far enough apart from the living room to have adequate square feet of its own for comfort, the round table and elegant chairs achieve dining-room status. What gives the setting its magic? The dazzling elongated chandelier, the painted furniture embellished with gold, and the mirror and glass that twinkle in the background. If you were to light candles on this table, all around you would see the glow reflected. Of course, the champagne-colored wood floor also does its part. A rug—even the best sort—would lessen the formality. And those large windows may be across the room, but the romance of city lights beyond the glass works a charm here, too.

Opposite: *Carefully edited furnishings heighten the drama of this dining room. The mirrored niches displaying artful ceramics interject light and serve as focal points. Observe how the wall curves, enhancing the sense of space, which is also what the mirrored door does for the scene.*

Architect: David Estreich; Designer: Gail Green

Marvelous Materials

Looking almost like a waterfall, a glass screen has been installed above a wood buffet to shield the dining table from the kitchen. With glass doors offering spectacular desert vistas right at their elbows and a ceiling that's fantastically raised above their heads, diners won't be distracted by what's happening at the stove. Tantamount to the architecture and the views, though, are the materials: a stone floor, steel-banded chairs, a modern metal light fixture, a glass-topped table, and granite layering the curved buffet. It's a full serving of interesting textures that makes the room memorable. The palette for finishes and fabrics is kept to colors that are reminiscent of the surroundings, and this helps to produce a serene atmosphere. And, for more serenity, note the curves: the buffet, the dining chairs, the upholstered seats in the living area, the round tables, and the ceiling dome. Not many sharp edges are here to jar a mood.

Left: *Resting above the stone floor, the table's round glass top appears light as air. According to experts, round tables are the best for a dinner party because everyone is included in the conversation. The rich hue of the chairs is coordinated with the color of the handy buffet.*

Right: *Every dining room should have a focal point this grand! Parking the table by the glass doors allows guests to enjoy the moonlit landscape. The metal in the lamps, the copper screen in the corner, and the chairs are all contemporary touches.*

Architect: Ron Robinette; Builder: Old Pueblo Remodelers; Designer: Lori Carroll, ASID, IIDA

Some meals you don't relish eating in the kitchen. On those occasions, you want the luxury of a room set aside specifically for great meals and conversation. This room takes its role seriously; so much thought has been given to comfort and practicality. On one side, the stunning wine rack shields the diners from the hubbub of the kitchen; on the other side, a marble-faced hearth separates the table from the living room. Since traffic can move freely around both these dividers, the dining room feels spacious and grand. A large bank of windows ushers in natural sunlight and moonlight for the pleasure of all. The Oriental carpet is the design's anchor. Offset by the black chairs, the carpet's colors interject heat into the otherwise cool setting. To facilitate serving, a convenient sideboard and an extra table are just right for staging luscious desserts and coffee.

Right: *The hearth separates the living and dining rooms without blocking either one. A lone painting, rather than a bevy of pictures, and no mantel foster a modern feel. Dimmers control the overhead lights, so the room can be brightened on demand.*

Left: *The built-in wine rack forms an attractive alcove for the sideboard. Although the sideboard's top is slated for serving, cupboard space below could be taken up with table linens. An Oriental rug filled with deep rich color is a good choice for a monochromatic room that doesn't want to look overdressed.*

If you prefer a spicy diet, a dining room that overflows with zest—from furnishings to fixtures—could fit the bill. Here, the whitewashed ceiling and massive beams make a delightful contrast with walls sponged a tropical blue. The cool backdrop is just what's needed to offset a palette that includes orange and hot yellows. The architecture of the space suggests a Southwestern motif, but European influences are here as well. Decorative paint draws all the elements— mismatched dining chairs, table, and armoires—together. But since the floor is also painted, the designer chose to leave the wood of the room's tall entry doors untouched. Like an oasis, the doors afford

Above: *A cupboard with glass doors is a fine addition for a dining room. Not only do you get to display your best dishes up above, but the storage down below is invaluable. And a hand-painted one like this is a special treat, because painted decoration transforms any piece into an artful treasure.*

a visual resting spot in the midst of the activity. The handsome counter separating the dining area from the cooking zone is another quiet surface. When the festive dinnerware is laid out, however, it's a delicious hot zone, too!

Left: *To add even more drama and excitement, each dining chair—although painted in the same colors—wears a different pattern along its seat and back. They are new, but the table is from the 19th century. Adding to the mix, an interesting hanging lamp stirs thoughts of India.*

The Spaniards may not have found gold when they explored the Southwest, but they left behind a treasure trove of rich cultural history. The Spanish influence looms large in this sunlit dining room. Look to the black wrought-iron chairs; the bare, light-reflecting floor; and the religious-themed art. Stripped down to essentials, the welcoming space conjures a feeling of intense light with color. The subtle play of shapes and materials is, however, what supplies visual interest. The curly-backed chairs, for example, act as an amusing foil to the square wood table's geometric fabric skirt. The furry cowhide rug and seat coverings are standard features in the Southwest, but coupled with a set of soft-flowing drapes, their casual demeanor subdues any hard edges. The drapes frame a doorway that leads to a companion sitting area. Take note of the clever continuation of the chair rail.

Right: *A painted chair rail breaks up the plane of the wall, dividing the bright yellow of the upper portion and the quiet, more creamlike tone of the lower wall. The inward-swinging casement windows are more dramatic minus inset curtains or drapes.*

Right: *Note how the chair rail subtly switches to a more decorative design and the wall colors are varied in the sitting area. The green plant, the ceramic pot, and the cow horns above the door are accessories that lend a Southwest note. Iron elements in each area help unify the rooms.*

Softness and Light

Aging paint finishes, gallons of white paint, and seagull-white slipcovers transform this small dining room into a wonderfully romantic setting. Trademarks of the popular "shabby chic" style, these unimposing ingredients are just right for today's casual living. The farmhouse table will withstand all sorts of wear and tear and be the better for it. And because color and pattern would have lessened the elegant, cool effect, walls and drapes are also white. Why, even the chandelier is ethereal. Unencumbered with a rug, the wood floor can show off its natural beauty. Placing the large table on the diagonal is a savvy decorating trick, too. Less an impediment to traffic moving in and out of the living room, the arrangement alters the look of a thin space by helping to expand the visual boundaries. Come nightfall when the candles are lit, the whole scene sparkles.

Right: *A medium-size platter is the center point for a collection of antique plates hung as art. The plate grouping also acts as a cap for the cupboard and helps to draw the eye up. Cutlery, linens, and extra candles could hide behind the wooden doors and in the drawers.*

Opposite: *A 12-inch-wide strip down the length of a table is ideal for decorating. For this occasion, a miniature bench raises the centerpiece. Although too high for dining, such a presentation is ideal for a buffet. The adjoining room features more white and sun-faded upholstery. Mostly white pottery lines the shelves.*

Identically framed ornithological studies have a huge impact on this traditional dining room. The sheer number of birds makes the walls grand focal points. Team the pictures with classic furniture, and the mood is elegant and refined. Matching lamps shed pools of light on a burnished sideboard, while candle-holding sconces and an elaborate chandelier lend a bit of theater. Rather than a plain white ceiling, a canopy of pale blue is a calming contrast with the cream-colored walls. If your own pocketbook won't stretch for expensive mattes and frames, consider inexpensive flea-market or craft-store frames spray-painted an identical color. A collection of botanical prints or old photographs will render an equally dramatic effect if the objects share similar hues. Include a scattering of silver and cut glass to heighten the formal mood. And choose white flowers—the most genteel blooms of all—when guests are due.

Left: *A silver urn looks smashing filled with white flowers. Mimic the look with an old silver trophy to hold garden flowers. Trophies or loving cups—often found at flea markets and tag sales—are considered collectibles. A twin set of pale blue lamps imitate the ceiling's luminous color.*

Right: *The architecture and formal symmetry of this dining room evoke an old-world stateliness. Limiting furnishings to just what's necessary also contributes to the sophisticated air as does the dark-stained floor.*

Left: *The not-formal, but not-overly-casual slipcovers are fashioned with a band of color along the hem. Such details lend stature to the simplest slipcovers or drapes. The woven basket, the horse, and the greens prevent the pale scene from slipping into too quiet a mood.*

Above: *To afford guests an extra bit of comfort, every straight-back chair holds a squishy pillow in a muted shade of green. Having taken on starfish as a theme, it's festive to offer cookies in that shape at party time. A flowerpot with a white patina is a complementary vessel for ranunculus.*

Designer: Drysdale & Associates Interior Design

Today's take on classic style translates into good architecture, a limited palette, and furnishings—some old, some new—that can hold their own. The shape of a table, for instance, is as important as the molding that surrounds the hearth. This beach house gets the formula just right: an antique table reinvented with white paint and a chorus of sprightly new dining chairs. The canvas slipcovers have been appliqued with starfish; the starfish play up the idea that this is a home by the sea and that it was designed for easy summer living. The ceiling-high French doors wear only the lightest wisp of a drape with a matching trim of humorous starfish, only this time they're scaled down. And the wide-plank floors remain bare—the better to deal with the occasional sand that finds its way in. Over the mantel, a trio of black-and-white photographs of beautiful destinations lends a graphic punch.

The restoration of an authentic gatehouse, now on the National Register of Historic Places, was an involved process that entailed years of hard work. The result, however, is a glorious, light-swept home filled with character and charm. Who would guess that the dining and living rooms were once horse stalls? The wainscoting and the wide-plank floors don't give a clue. And, certainly, the squares of stained glass tucked in each window could not have had such humble beginnings? To maintain the unique character of the 140-year-old structure, the interior design focused on traditional New England antiques. The pale walls were chosen to keep the rooms looking airy and open, which is exactly how dinner guests perceive it when they see the old building for the first time. The simple furnishings let the house tell its story, and from hay and horses to beautiful home, it's quite a tale.

Opposite: *The most telling signs of the home's history are original hay baskets in the corners of the dining room. A sturdy painted table and a regiment of antique chairs accommodate a number of people. Guests seated at the table look across the living room and out the new glass doors.*

Left: *A love for all things Victorian lead to an antique sofa and armchair that have been rebuilt for comfort. Antique wicker chairs were given a revamp with a coat of green paint. Original barn doors frame the new French doors. And Majolica plates pick up on the chair's garden color.*

Designer: Susan Thorn Interior Design

The creamy colored walls and wood floor in this French-country-influenced room readily adapt to the major furniture pieces: a glass-topped dining table with a hefty travertine base and twin arched-top china cabinets. Flanking the window, the cabinets play up the space's lofty ceiling; while the dishware on display inside the cabinets interjects subtle color. Around the table, a half dozen upholstered chairs contribute comfort. Add an elaborate triple-tier chandelier, a needlepoint rug in muted shades, and some handsome art, and all your guests will want to dress up for dinner. Although at its best when the table is set as it is here with a collection of antique china and clear and cobalt stemware, the room maintains its character even when not called into service. Spied from the living room through a gracious arch, it's the kind of dining room that enhances an entire house with its regal presence.

Above: *A custom-designed travertine and metal console repeats the theme of the travertine-based dining table. In keeping with a French mood, the drapes are simple but sophisticated. Hung slightly higher than the glass, they appear to enlarge the opening.*

Right: *A travertine wall shelf is balanced on the other side of the dining room with a lean console. The shelf cleverly provides additional space for serving but doesn't impact the square footage. Fabric shades soften the light from the brass chandelier.*

Designer: Joseph P. Horan, FASID

Totally original, this captivating dining room brings together traditional and ethnic pieces. The comfortable upholstered chairs, for instance, would look just as at home in a classic setting. The elaborate chandeliers, however, make us think of an Indian bazaar. To keep the elements in balance, rose-colored walls are met with pale trim and woodwork. The walls' rich color adds depth to the space, making it appear more opulent and cozy even on the chilliest of evenings. On one side of the gleaming table, a baronial hearth is the dining room's focal point. On the other, an ornate mirror catches the eye by enhancing the light during the day and also when the candles are aglow. The most memorable rooms usually feature a surprise component, and there's one here. Should the guests raise their eyes to the ceiling, they'll discover, much to their delight, a decorative pattern rather than a mundane white canopy.

Right: *Beautiful but simple vases stand guard on the narrow console. Although the room has sumptuous appointments, there's a subtlety in the overall design. One outstanding mirror, for instance, is more effective than a wall full of art.*

Opposite: *Painting the ceiling the same hue as the walls imbues the room with a more intimate ambience. The alluring rosy red color also helps highlight the decoration. Formal drapes would not have been inappropriate, but the light-giving sheers are far less overpowering and offer a softer look.*

Designer: Kari Whitman

Bedrooms That Beckon

Master bedrooms are not just spaces where we go to slumber. They are relaxing havens where we can examine the day's events and retreat into a meditative and inquisitive state.

Do you want your bedroom to be a Zen-like sanctuary filled with soothing neutral tones or a French provincial bonbon? Make it the bedroom of your dreams with a sleep-inducing bed, adequate storage, and good lighting. Include family photographs, a TV, a sound system, a desk—whatever makes you content.

Follow the experts' counsel: Expand a tight room with light colors and filmy curtains, and cozy up a big room with warm tones (such as raspberry or periwinkle) and patterns (such as gingham, toile, or stripes). To make the most of every foot of space, station bigger pieces of furniture parallel or perpendicular to the walls.

No matter whether you choose funky mismatched nightstands or the pair that came in your bedroom suite, be sure they are as high as the top of the mattress. You don't want to have to fumble in the dark for the phone or your alarm clock. Boost a boring nightstand set by including a quirky flea-market find such as an old chest to hold extra blankets. A miniature muslin bag stuffed with rosemary or lavender will prevent

mustiness and keep a chest, drawer, or linen closet smelling fresh. Attractive, qual-

ity linens will ensure a heavenly rest.

KIDS' ROOMS

From nursery to preteen, it happens fast! Choose neutral colors and wallpaper that

will adapt as the child grows. In lieu of bunnies, use a small-print wallpaper. Rather

than buy furnishings that are age-specific, look for pieces that will endure, such

as a rocker or armoire. The armoire can hold toys now, electronic gear later. If you're

remodeling, install childproof electrical outlets for future use. Built-in bookcases and

dressers provide lasting storage. Shelves, window seats with pullout drawers or lift-up

seats, and cubbyholes can serve as storage.

Shaker pegs and plastic bins also instill order.

Designate a vinyl confetti-print floor that

resists scuff marks as the play area, and a comfy

island of carpet with a ton of floor pillows as a

place for quiet pursuits. Rather than floor or

table lamps that might take up a lot of space

and end up getting knocked down, look to wall sconces and recessed lighting. Framed maps,

antique animal prints, and posters will generate visual interest without being babyish.

TEENS' ROOMS

Create a private hangout for your teen using the teen's favorite colors and sensible fur-

nishings. A bed is the center of their universe; it's where they talk on the phone and

lounge with friends. Opt for comfortable simple bedding like a

duvet and a minimum number of pillows to encourage bed-

making. Twin beds are practical for sleep-overs and, painted the

same color, need not match. Upholster the headboards, or dec-

orate them with stencils. Mismatched but coordinating linens

will keep separate beds looking upbeat. Try yellow-and-white-

checked sheets with a red bedskirt on one bed, for example, and red-and-white-checked

sheets with a yellow skirt on the other. Wallcoverings that mimic decorative painting

techniques or their favorite fabric, such as denim, are also cool in girls' or boys' rooms.

Call in modular units customized with shelves and drawers, a flea-market desk refur-

bished with paint, or an antique table as a workstation. Install shelves nearby to hold

books and papers. A large bulletin board is a good catchall for photos and sports sched-

ules. And an ergonomically designed office chair is a healthy choice for a young back.

GUEST ROOMS

Necessities for guests include a comfortable bed, a good reading light, a place for clothes (a portion of the closet, an antique coat rack, or a stretch of simple Shaker pegs), and privacy. For entertainment, move in a tiny television, a compact disc player, and a stack of magazines. A pretty drinking glass on a tray by the bed, a basket of fresh fruit for late-night nibbling, and a soft throw are welcoming extras. And don't forget a stack of plump towels.

If your home doesn't allow space for a full-time guest abode, consider a sleeping area in your home office with a modular unit that features a fold-down bed. Additional creative solutions include boat- or railcar-style berths, faithful futons, and the summer winner, an enclosed porch. Delicate sheers hung on rods in front of the porch screens or yards of diaphanous muslin suspended above the bed will enhance the fanciful feeling of sleeping outdoors.

Left: *A sitting area transforms a bedroom into a sanctuary. The traditional wing chairs look up to date since they are upholstered in off-white. Marble—the same color as the carpet—is an upgrade for a low-key hearth.*

Your bedroom should suit your personality. If you are a traditionalist at heart but prefer your interiors carefully edited and somewhat casual, a room like this should be a match. The snowy linens and the easy-to-do window treatment emphasize that this is a room where dreams are made. The dark wood furnishings against the soothing palette of creams and white display their shapes to best advantage. But what's included here is only what's needed: an inviting bed for dreaming, a mirrored armoire to hold clothing and electronics, and two very comfortable wing chairs where you and yours can sit and relax. The porcelain, pottery, and art bring forth just a hint of color to complement the sea view. And there's a bit of architectural detailing to add character to the simple white mantel. Soft wall-to-wall carpeting pampers bare feet.

Opposite: *The sleigh bed is situated by the window so occupants can watch the waves. A large mirror reflects the view for optimum pleasure. A bit of lace on sheets and table scarves and a luxurious fringed throw prevent the setting from appearing sterile.*

Designer: Janet Brown

The color blue relaxes and refreshes, making it the ultimate color for a bedroom. The pale wood floor is also a good choice; it opens the small room visually and collects the light. Contemporary furnishings are low-key and fitting, but the window treatment is a surprise. Beneath the wide blue valance unfolds the sheerest of sheers. The feminine curtains are layered over blue drapes that pull neatly to the side during the day so as not to interfere with the sun. It's a sumptuous dressing, but it's also young and fresh like a prom dress or a corsage. Along this same whimsical vein, the iron bed is full of curves. And—look up—a spiral pendant lamp shade is covering what was previously a ho-hum light fixture. A little bit of fantasy here and there hasn't minimized the modern look. On the contrary, it's just made it charming.

Right: *More yin and yang: A portly slipcovered armchair cozies up to a metal and glass table. The geometric candleholder and the curly mini-lamp were chosen for their interesting forms.*

Opposite: *A pair of wood bureaus with metal trim balances the mighty bed, and their clean lines keep the room feeling up to date. Pillows—always a welcome addition when it's time to rest or read—soften the metal. The intriguing wall sconce adds a warm glow when night falls.*

Swedish Sorbet

A white-and-yellow scheme, although not as well recognized as the traditional blue-and-white mix, is a Swedish favorite. Given a large injection of white—walls, ceiling, and floor—this room is inviting without being cloying. The arresting concoction of patterns and textures steps up the tiny retreat's energy level and catches your attention. The fleur-de-lis pattern on the rug, for instance, creates an elevated background for a simple wicker daybed that has been loaded with plump pillows. The rug's color and design is also an interesting juxtaposition with the wide white-and-yellow stripes on the wall. Summer or winter, a cheerful decor like this can host either traditional or country elements. For a more contemporary spin, though, consider a durable sisal rug, and edit your accessories. Remember, yellow is a perfect color when you need to brighten a small room that's short on natural daylight.

Left: *This pert slipper chair with its tassel trim is a comfortable and stylish addition. Teamed with a decoratively painted stand, it helps to create a sweet vignette. Flowers are a strong motif in this petite bedroom, appearing on everything from the lamp to furniture.*

Right: *Prominent against the sunny hues are a number of botanicals. The trio of flowers framed in checks on the door is particularly arresting. Simple flourishes like a smart bedskirt take an ordinary wicker daybed to new heights. And wicker and wainscoting are an age-old recipe that never fails to please.*

Designer: Gail Green/
Green & Co.

This beautifully composed room, with its dark and boldly carved Colonial-style furniture, will never be out of style. Although incorporating global influences is a currently popular trend, all the elements here are handled in a controlled and timeless manner. The zebra-skin rug, for example, and the Asian-inspired woven baskets add to the setting but don't monopolize our attention. What does garner a second look? The handsome bed with its abundance of well-planned coverings and pillows, the romantic chandelier with its glass shades, and the architecture itself. From the detailed ceiling to the trio of French doors that serve as windows, the room exudes elegance. Cognizant of its built-in charm, the owners abandoned patterns and opted instead for simple curtains, a casual sisal carpet, and walls the color of milky coffee. A plain rattan chair—rather than an ornate upholstered seat—maintains the proper mood and affords an extra place to sit or dream.

Right: *A leggy lamp illuminates a carefully choreographed vignette atop the polished bureau. Chic but simple upholstery with a palm tree theme is in keeping with the room's island air. Flowing drapes are an additional sophisticated touch.*

Manufacturer:
Thomasville Furniture

Left: *A pristine white ceiling and white trim imbues the space with a fresh edge. Angling the bed affords more space for moving about. Small treasures such as seashells gathered from a favorite beach are additional charm enhancers.*

T his bedroom exudes lay-down-and-rest-awhile vibes. The pared-down venue and the soothing combination of colors—predominately earthy browns, beiges, and creams—has a lulling, soothing quality. Windows on two sides of the room are an architectural plus; to capitalize on their presence, simple shades have been installed in lieu of curtains or shutters. The shots of red—the armchairs, the shades on the sconces, the flowers—are small wake-up calls that cheer the scene without lessening the stream-lined aesthetic. Modern furnishings that match each other in style and look comple-ment the mostly bare walls and the glowing wood floor. And, the carpet livens things up. Its pattern is peppy but not so vibrant that we are distracted from the peacefulness of the room. There is a clock, but when in this room, it's always sleepy time.

Left: *Only two paint-ings (another is over the dresser) grace the walls. Even the lamps—plain white—have a demure pres-ence. Bed linens bring out the purple in the paintings, and bedside tables are kept bare. Such neatness adds to comforting minimalism.*

Above: *This composition of color and light is a pleasing spectacle. The symmetry of the windows, of the metal-legged chairs, and of the light fixtures contributes to the room's serene air. The area rug centers the design and adds a touch of comfort.*

Sleepy Time

This beguiling French provincial bedroom has an upbeat atmosphere that speaks to our country's often practical, less romantic nature. For example, the bed's curvy shape and floral covering in a sun-warmed shade of yellow are traditional. And, so is the lighthearted blend of supportive pillow fabrics. But, the two striped patterns (horizontal and vertical) that dress the windows and glass doors are modern and straightforward. Instead of painted furniture in light tones like that which is often seen in this type of room, the decorative finish on the wall-mounted cupboard, nightstand, and desk is a watery blue to match the come-hither chair snuggling in the corner. In step with our newest determination to pare down to essentials, polished wood floors are left bare and accessories are minimized—no urns or artifacts, just family pictures and well-loved knickknacks. Foregoing a beautiful chandelier, too, the owners have opted for functional wall-mounted lamps.

Above: *An assembly of colors taken from an Impressionist's palette says French loud and clear. The decoratively painted night table garners extra praise with its snappy checkerboard display. At the windows, subtle shears on rods are gathered so they stay where they're wanted.*

Left: *A fireplace in a bedroom is the ultimate luxury. A fanciful mirror suspended above the mantel makes the hearth even more lovely. Sweet collectibles and photographs look right at home on shelves given new personality with imaginative carved moldings.* Right: *Blue-and-yellow striped drapes—vertical beside the bed, horizontal at the glass doors— are a fresh addition to a bouquet of French-like flowery patterns. The eye focuses on the architecture since there isn't a painting over the bed. The wall-mounted cupboard houses collectibles in a safe manner.*

Designer: Dennis Jenkins

Feminine Mystique

Bring together the elements that you love, and miraculously, they will all merge to fashion a room that is both personal and pretty. That was the idea in this eclectic bedroom, and the alluring results are a testament to how well the strategy works. Favoring the cool, clean Swedish look, the space relies heavily on white—furnishings, fabrics, and walls—to relay a restful mood. The splash of yellow on the wall behind the bed helps to frame the sleeping area and showcase the blue-and-white components: the mound of come-and-rest pillows and the trio of sweet porcelain plates. For textural interest, the owners have chosen an architectural fragment for above the bed and pretend pilasters. Their distressed finished is a fine partner to a pristine chenille bedspread and a chenille-covered stool where a porcelain cat rests. Layering an area rug with a blue blossom border over the wall-to-wall carpeting adds richness.

Left: *An old wicker table and a simple chair have been given a romantic bent with a variety of snowy-colored coverings. Along with a chandelier and a gauzy window treatment that incorporates a ribbon of miniature lights, it's a scene straight from a fairy tale. The blue-and-white teacup sculpture is a whimsical accessory.*

Right: *White paint and a distressed finish transform an ordinary trunk into a worthy object. Inside, blankets find a home. The iron bed has also been left as-is since its patina is part of its charm. Mismatched frames and mirrors bring a kind of quirky elegance to the setting.*

These two bedrooms take a similar approach to comfort. Their layout might be different, but the result is the same: an inviting haven for resting and relaxing. In one, the beds are smartly laid head to head against the wall, and that increases the amount of floor space for dressing and moving about. In the other, the beds flank opposite sides of an elevated area that claims one end of the room. Both solutions boast bountiful built-in storage so that two people can share either of these inviting spaces and have plenty of room for clothes and gear. The decoratively carved and painted frames that incorporate the storage also enhance the charm. Crawling under the covers, sleepers can imagine they're on a boat or, perhaps, in a tree house. The unpainted wood walls and ceilings evoke outdoor thoughts that are readily conducive to sleep and to sweet dreams for adults or children.

Opposite: *Convenient built-in shelving helps make the most of the sleeping area. Occupants have a secure place to rest books, a lamp, and the telephone. A long tapestry hung creatively along the wall above the beds renders the nest homier.*

Left: *Bring on the texture: Rough-hewn walls and paneled ceilings help make the room romantic and intriguing. For practicality, drawers have been positioned at the end of each bed for easy access.*

Wallpaper transforms a room optically by pushing the walls out or the ceiling up, creating the illusion of more space. Here, a classic blue-and-white combination renders a simple bedroom majestic. Matching fabric and wallpaper is a continuation of the 18th-century style of applying similar fabric on walls and at windows. Many fashionable French interiors during that time, for instance, included furniture, walls, and curtains all covered in the same fabric. The large amount of white here, though, gives the room a cleaner, more modern edge. The simple blue-and-white rug is also a fresh take and provides a contemporary balance to the classic paper. Multiple patterns in the same palette range are another update. The pillow coverings and seat cushion support the theme but introduce touches of yellow, green, and rose, all soft flower colors with a bit of energy so the room looks classy but current.

Left: *The white bed-covering is a breath of spring air that tempers the busyness of the paper and fabric. Traditional furniture and a few well-chosen accents of gold denote elegance without appearing too heavy-handed. Matching lamps with a bird theme are a clever addition above each bedside table.*

Above: *Multiple patterns such as the slipcover on the chaise and the pillow coverings take the room in a new direction. The folding screen also contributes interest with its picturesque blue-and-white scene. A one-colored pattern, toile makes an interesting backdrop for pictures and decorative furnishings.*

Designers: Michael Whaley Interiors, Inc.

Green Peace

Above: *The handsome moldings in this room dictated more formal window treatments. But during daylight hours, elegant tie-backs hold the generously wide drapes to one side so the light can pour in. Foregoing ordinary reading lamps, the owners opted for stately fixtures that would double as art objects.*

In these busy times, your bedroom should be your haven. To fashion a composition that promotes tranquility begin with the background as these clever owners have done. The color green is recognized by experts as having a soothing meditativeness that keeps us feeling in touch with nature. Building on a theme of relaxation and serenity, the owners selected blonde furniture, which is less jarring than dark wood, and neutral fabrics, rather than busy patterns, to conjure the quotient of elegance they desired. To play up the handsome windows, drapes have been teamed with tailored valances. These formal treatments deliver an extra punch of luxury as does the handsome upholstered headboard on the bed. Wall-to-wall carpeting helps muffle sounds and makes the room appear visually larger as does the lack of cozy clutter. Plenty of closed storage keeps a slick room such as this looking organized and beautiful around the clock.

Right: *A bold bed sets the tone for this pared-down but handsome space. At the bed's foot, a fat ottoman with a pert skirt serves as a seat or an extra table. Matching armchairs and nightstands increase the bedroom's level of formality.*

Little girls love pink, and big girls do, too. Still, cognizant that the occupant of this pleasingly rosy room will need a space that matures along with her, a wallcovering that isn't age-specific was chosen. The tiny star pattern will be a fine background even when the storybooks and dolls are moved out. White furniture is another savvy decision. Timeless in their appeal, the white dresser and bed can stay right where they are forever. The drapes are soft and feminine and also not in the least babyish. Paired with crisp white shutters, in fact, the drapes offer a small princess a hint of enduring elegance. The gold-framed prints that adorn the wall above the bookcase also interject some sophistication. As the years go by, the collection can be added to; as it grows so will its sentimental value until it's as well-loved as a favorite cuddly teddy bear.

Right: *A cheerful—not overly little-girlish— slipcover makes a comfy armchair a pal no matter what the owner's age. The decoratively painted bookcase shares the slipcover's pattern. Custom touches such as this give a young child's or teen's room extra flair.*

Opposite: *Bows on the bedcovering are echoed by the lamp shade's decoration. Louvered shutters let in light but guard privacy. And fabric sleeves shirred on to the curtain rods add style. For lounging with friends or simply stretching out with a book, soft but durable wall-to-wall carpeting is the solution.*

Designer: Carol R. Knott

Above: *Deep fringe increases a tufted armchair's importance. In a similar vein, hefty brass rods installed almost at ceiling height give ordinary windows a dash of elegance. Our lesson? Details always count.*

Above: *Hidden within the alluring clouds are words and pictures that are meaningful to the owners. White doves—one in flight, the other perched on the edge of the recessed ceiling—capture the eye and the imagination.*

Designer: Darla Blake, ASID, CID

No one can promise that a beautiful vista overhead will make getting up in the morning any easier. But, certainly, it couldn't hurt. The owners of this bedroom wake to a mural composed of swirling clouds and bright blue sky every day. The showstopping ceiling has transformed their average-size retreat into a unique room with a magical quality all its own. The iron bed may be contemporary in flavor, but the haven's palette of colors and the sensuous display of fabrics—from gathered bedskirt to draperies—lend a decidedly old-world feeling. Adding to the grandeur, oversize, hand-painted European chests of drawers cleverly fill in as nightstands, while a heap of comfy pillows and several soft-to-the-touch throws increase tactile interest and warmth. A decoratively painted armoire and cabinet also subtly heighten the mood. And an Oriental rug, laid atop the wall-to-wall carpet, injects color and more texture at the room's heart.

Right: *The bedskirt and the bed's fetching ribbon-like canopy are rendered in matching fabric for unity. To draw attention to the bed's seductive modern shape, art is hung at the side where the iron headboard dips. A large painting above one nightstand is balanced with a grouping of art above the other.*

This is most certainly a lady's chambers. Although this bedroom is very feminine, it could also accommodate a man. The meticulous attention to details makes it less froufrou and more elegantly Swedish. To conjure a similar ambience in your bedroom, look to a combination of blue and white, light-painted furnishings, and accents of gold, be it mirrors, picture frames, lamps, or a dainty foot stool you gild yourself. The marriage on the wall of decorative paint and paper makes the high-ceilinged room more inviting by shortening the wall. And the repeated use of pattern—on the window seat, the upholstered bed, and the generous balloon shade—also helps to cozy up the space. Still, the magnificent painted ceiling is the icing on the cake. It's no coincidence that the rug—layered over the sisal carpet—is almost a match. Details are what makes this grand bedroom so remarkable and so very pretty.

Above: *The figure on the wall plaque is repeated on the chair; such repetitive choreography unifies this large space. An upholstered bench at the bed's foot is a staple in traditional bedrooms. This one is Gustavian to honor the room's style.*

Above: *Framed panels hung as art echo the wallcovering. The sisal carpet acts as a hardwood floor lending cohesion. Lucky is the bird who gets to sing in the wedding-cakelike birdcage, a romantic addition that suits the window seat's arched ceiling.*

Above: *Simple shapes, symmetry, and painted woods speak to the look. Here, twin gold mirrors and lamps are offset with mismatched nightstands, each of which is almost at the same height as the other. An upholstered bed is luxurious. Small touches—a candle and photographs—are ways to warm a similar room, but clutter should be avoided.*

Architect: David Estreich; Designer: Gail Green

A Fish Tale

Choosing a theme is often a productive way to launch a decorating project. Here, for instance, the focus is fish. Look how they swim not only across the dresser but also on the walls and the pillows. Not overly masculine, though, this room is a great catch for either gender. The rustic stone walls and leaded windows invoke thoughts of romantic stone cottages hidden in the country. Against the cool gray, the sunny bed-covering is an island of warmth, a place you might gladly snuggle all day. The woven rattan chair is also a smart foil for the rugged architecture. And notice how the floor is cozied up with not just one carpet, but a creative layering of two diverse rugs. Bring in a large mirror in an interesting folk art frame to increase the light and a bouquet of fresh, smell-delicious flowers, and it's a timeless, feel-good getaway.

Left: *A could-have-been-ordinary dresser becomes a treasure embellished with fanciful fish. If you're not a talented artist and would like to try your hand, consider a stencil to achieve a similar effect. Old leather-bound books and carved birds help personalize the setting.*

Manufacturer:
Thomasville Furniture

Above: *A white-painted nightstand would have complemented the dresser but also would have been redundant. The unpainted piece is a far more interesting choice teamed with the iron bed. The folding screen behind the bed alters the shape of the room and softens the scene.*

Dream-Catcher

This fascinating room packs a supercharged amount of globally inspired design appeal into a relatively small space. If you're at a loss as to what to do with your own bedroom, study the drama that unfolds within these walls. And what walls! The story begins with their hot, persimmon-colored surface, which is repeated in the bed covering, the silk pillows, and the sunburstlike light fixture. The sea-grass rug tempers the warmness and so do the sheers, which drop like wings at each window. Silvery candleholders also interject a bit of coldness (and spiritually raise the energy level). But everything else—the ottoman, the pottery dishes, and the lacquered trays—basks in the heat. The bedroom becomes even more exotic with the collection of stones—each set in an individual dish—and the interesting African-like stools and sculpture. You might catch a dream in a bedroom like this—of another world!

Opposite: The dark wall behind the bed helps to set the resting area apart. Against its cloudy surface, the wall-hanging sculpture is also better observed. The dark wooden bench at the foot of the bed is used as a display area rather than as a traditional seat.

Right: *The window seat is lined with dainty bolsters that gently define individual sitting areas. An assortment of lovely stones inspires meditation and prayer. Since privacy is not an issue, the filmy drapes are more than enough to cover the windows.*

Designer: Stacey Lapuk, ASID, CID

Baths, Big and Small

In general, all baths—from the luxurious spa to the cheerful, kid-friendly bath down the hall—require adequate light, good ventilation, plenty of storage, and fittings and fixtures that are as practical as they are attractive. Traditionally styled fixtures and fittings are featured in a wide range of prices so it's possible to achieve a high-end look without paying a fortune. Savvy homeowners who might not have the budget for a marble floor, say, can opt for faux-marble ceramic tiles and still get the look.

Spaciousness is a luxury in itself. But small retreats can also be indulgent. Go wholly modern, traditional, or somewhere delightfully in between. Each of the three fundamental areas—the bathing and showering area, the sink and grooming area, and the toilet

area—should be planned with your particular habits and tastes in mind. Safety measures like grab bars, no-scald faucets, rounded corners on counters, and slip-resistant surfaces benefit all ages and abilities. Thoughtful touches like a shaving mirror mounted above the sink, towel warmers, and handheld showers are always appreciated additions.

Master baths, guest-room baths, and powder rooms tend to be more opulent than family or children's baths. With safety in mind, the last kind needs to be planned to grow along with the kids. Simple neutral palettes and straightforward cabinetry that can be painted or stained as tastes mature are ideal. Built-in storage that provides drawers as well as cubbies for towels will look adorable now and years down the road.

To facilitate traffic in a busy family bath, consider installing a separate tub and shower (an angled shower makes use of a corner). Design a countertop that extends the length of the room and uses

varying widths to create a useful surface that will leave floor space open. A private enclosure for the toilet will be a boon when kids and parents are rushing, too. Choose light-reflective materials such as maple cabinets, stainless-steel sinks, and polished-chrome faucets to keep a contemporary bath looking airy. White wainscoting and white brick tile will have a similar dazzling effect in a traditional room.

For organization, build in a vented laundry hamper beside the sink. If a child needs a step stool to reach the faucets, find one that folds up and away when not in use. Hang hooks at a level to accommodate each family member's robe, and allot each member a shelf or a drawer.

What they lack in size, powder rooms more than make up with usability. Strategically placed beside an office or den, these little rooms—with usually just a sink and

toilet—can serve as guest baths. If yours is located close to a formal living room, duplicate the living room's style with faux-finished wall treatments and gold or brass fixtures. Consider paneling or go wild with color and flea-market finds for a basement powder room. An iron shelf to hang above a pedestal sink? A retro plastic chair teamed with colored tiles?

A sanctuary designed for two should strive to suit both parties. In addition to dual sinks (which could be back to back as well as side by side), plan separate recessed medicine cabinets. Install vanities at comfortable heights, and include twin dressing rooms. Experiment with materials, colors, and textures for a unique look that expresses your style. A grand skylight or windows beside the tub and in the shower will allow you to commune with nature and leave your troubles behind.

Art Deco Delight

Modern and dramatic, the art deco style was a winner in the '20s and '30s. First taking hold in Europe, the style quickly crossed the Atlantic where we gave it even more of a streamlined look. Metallic finishes, geometric patterns, and bold designs— chevrons, zigzags, and stylized flowers—were hot. Whether you envision a full room or just a few touches of art deco, the style's clean-lined appearance can be a good partner for a modern or even an older home. Colors are a large part of the look. Most often, walls are white or off-white to provide a backdrop for accents of colors such as yellow, lime-green, and red. For more sophistication, however, choose a dramatic color scheme like shiny black and white. By the '30s, tubs were beginning to be boxed in. Still, this stylish bath on legs works with the color scheme and allows more black tile to be displayed. What else to be chic? A satisfying serving of shiny chrome!

Right: Gleaming black and white tile is appropriate for the art deco look. Adhering to the theme, the simply draped curtain is also white with touches of black. The shiny chrome rod adds one more bit of glitter.

Left: Originally, sinks from this period often stood on chrome legs with a rack attached for a towel (you can look for reproductions or check out salvage yards). The same effect is achieved here with the wall-mounted chrome towel rack. The fan-shaped mirror with its chrome touches and glass shelf is in sync.

Baths used to be designated only as functional spots for everyday ablutions and grooming. All that has changed with recent times. Now, we want our baths—no matter what style or size—to be sanctuaries, too. This cheerful room illustrates how easy it is to create an environment that will please you morning and night. A quirky wave of yellow and blue random-shaped tile, for example, is a fun and inexpensive backsplash for a standard pedestal sink. The sunny-colored wall also comes into play making this area a bright little oasis. Across the room, the wall color shifts to blue and a similar burst of tile appears behind the toilet. Pristine white woodwork tethers the two colors (one warm, one cool) so the overall effect is agreeable not haphazard. A wall shelving unit filled with toiletries and supplies—and including interesting objects like a clock and a miniature sailboat—reinforces the bath's happy-going personality.

Above: *In addition to the tile backsplash, similar tile was laid along the window ledge to form a durable and appealing waterproof area for toothbrushes and shaving supplies. A good-size mirror enhances the bath's light.*

Left: *The wall shelving unit gains stature by stepping up several inches on a tiled ledge. Here, white tiles tie in with the white wood-work and fixtures. The wispy drapes are also given a boost with a stylish black iron rod.*

Serene and welcoming, this bath is a masterly designed sanctuary inviting you to linger. Asian influences provide soothing ambience and the subtle blending of tactile materials, such as the handsome wood vanity and the woven baskets along with the stone tiles. Private courtyards allow the room to gather light and garden views from both the tub and the shower. With such stunning access to the outdoors, the monochromatic bath requires little else. The play of natural light across the surface of the stone changes the shadows and enhances the tranquil mood, and this mood is deepened with white flowers in full bloom and soft towels. Decorative accessories are limited to a few striking wall-mounted pieces to maintain the correct clean and uncluttered face. And the toilet has been slid away to rest in its own compartment. This glorious—and practical—bath promises rejuvenation of the spirit and that's what makes it successful.

Above: *Laying claim to its own private space, the toilet remains out of view. Such a plan also makes the bathroom more feasible for two to share. The plain-front vanity adds warmth to the stone in addition to supplying needed storage. Gleaming brass fixtures pick up the light.*

Left: *Someone in the bathtub or the stone shower can enjoy this large wonderful window through which light flows all day. Without a door and separated only by glass, the walk-in shower feels like it's a part of the garden. Built-in niches are convenient ways to keep soaps and shampoo within easy reach.*

Left: *The stepped surround leading to the deep soaking tub is another gesture to make the bathing experience more than just your usual grooming ritual. Over the interior window— which looks through glass doors to the sunlit garden—a parade of elephants is under way.*

Black-framed art is a modern touch in a room that's traditional in tone. Combining strong points of classic and contemporary design, this bath captures the divine style of old-world elegance without coming across as being stodgy. On the contrary, all the fixtures from the whirlpool and toilet to the sink exude a high-style profile that's just right for today's architecture. White fixtures endure, remember, no matter how tastes may change. Toss in a handful of gleaming chrome accents and a pearly gray marble floor for a bit of elegance, and the recipe is complete. The soft green walls may whisper that this is a space very much in step with the times, but green in one shade or another has never been out of style. And on top of all this good design, there's the light. Every bath benefits from natural light, and this one, with an undressed window, has more than its fair share.

Right: *A simple palette of two colors, one being a large amount of white, imbues the room with a polished demeanor. Against such a canvas, touches of black and chrome appear energized. The pair of low-slung black benches perform as seats or tables according to your whim.*

Right: *To master this look in your own home, limit accessories and consider classically designed fixtures that offer modern bonuses. This acrylic whirlpool tub, for instance, has individually adjustable jets to enhance the hydro-massage experience.*

Manufacturer: Kohler Co.

Texture overrules ornamentation in this room. The smooth grain of the bath's wood cabinets and the frosted-glass shower enclosure have a natural drama that doesn't require excessive fixtures. The large-size floor tiles also interject interest with their restful and subdued mixture of colors. Smoky gray and beige, like pebbles washed ashore, the tiles have a serene character evocative of leisurely strolls along a beach. High windows in the bathing area let in the light while preserving the owners' privacy. To safeguard the feeling of harmony, clutter is not allowed. Instead, the bath is equipped with plenty of storage that also acts as part of the design. Two grooming areas, each arranged with a mirror, allow a couple to share the space without battling for elbow room. The vanity area, though, includes a small magnifying mirror that makes it even more beneficial during daily grooming.

Left: *Continuing the hazy-hued tiles as a tub surround lends a woodland feel to the bathing area. Resting in the warm water, a bather can lean back and see the treetops through the high windows. Modern light fixtures are suitable for the room's clean-lined minimalist decor.*

Right: *The bath's quiet mood also stems from the comforting, neutral shade of the walls and the ceiling. Closely identified today with Asian styles of decorating, the pale colors are thought to give the mind time to dream and relax. Towels in the same color family blend rather than jar the setting.*

Architect: Hank Bruce, A/A; Designer: Jean Kezeor, ASID

Above: *Highly functional universal bathroom fixtures foster a gracious lifestyle while providing easy access. There's plenty of room, for instance, for knee and toe clearance at these handsome sinks. Easy-to-operate wing handled faucets are also helpful. Grab bars are an additional safety feature, and of course, adequate lighting is a must.*

Opposite: *Grab bars mounted near the toilet, around the tub, and in the shower are especially designed to support at least 250 lbs., making these fixtures accessible to people of various physical abilities. A stool stationed at the sink and storage units on casters so they can roll are thoughtful and wise additions.*

Manufacturer: Kohler Co.

It's not enough for a bath to be beautiful. For you and your family, you want a bath that is also safe. The National Kitchen and Bath Association (NKBA) has a number of guidelines to help you design a room that will assure livability for the young and the old as well as those people who may have special physical needs. Handy grab bars, wider doorways, and whirlpool tubs with fold-down seats, for example, are three "universal access" benefits that will be smart today and for all the years to come. But that's not to say you have to sacrifice style. Lavatories that offer the convenience of countertop installation while permitting full wheelchair accessibility, say, can be as stunning as this bath proves. Tiles with a nonslip finish are forever appealing, especially when their color is one of the new cheery citrus-greenish-yellow tones so currently popular.

Left: *An easy-to-manipulate shower head (which can also be used as a handheld shower), grab bars, and ample floor space for a wheelchair render this modern roll-in shower accessible to all. For additional safety protection, make certain faucets also feature scald protection.*

Less Is More

A pleasing harmony of past and present is achieved in this dark-floored, roomy bath. The new streamlined fixtures call to mind designs from the '20s and '30s. But incorporated in this white-on-white space, the fixtures take on an understated contemporary tone. For furnishings, the owners looked to simple pieces that would complement the pale beadboard paneling and add interest simultaneously. For example: A dark-stained wooden ladder steps in as decoration and also to hold extra towels, a tiny wooden stool becomes a tub-side table, and a woven basket hides supplies. Rather than the traditional white medicine cabinet, this one has gone dark—a fine contrast to the brilliant walls. Still, the focal point is the bathing area with its surplus of windows. Simple sheers, which are in demand now as part of the 21st-century urge to pare down, diffuse the light and help make the tub an oasis of serenity.

Left: *Reminiscent of a gallery in its starkness, a white bathroom forms a dazzling backdrop for antique, reproduction, or vintage pieces. Combining modern and traditional elements in an eclectic fashion is an excellent way to harvest the best of both worlds. Here, an old painted chair makes itself at home.*

Right: *Encased in beadboard, the deep tub becomes an integral part of the design. Scaling back on the tub surround, the owners opted to use a stool for keeping toiletries in close proximity. The lean glass shelf above the toilet also makes way for lotions and cologne without drawing attention.*

Manufacturer: Kohler Co.

Above: *At the small vanity, a hand-painted striped sink, an array of luscious tile, and a traditional faucet vie for attention. Wrapping the tile backsplash around the wall is a functional and stylish move. A casual roll-up fabric shade at the large window also interjects a bit of jewel-toned color.* Opposite: *What might have been a quirky pattern of colors comes across in this bath as very posh. In the dark, grottolike room, the vibrant tile floor and the confetti design of the vanity doors are light-catching. A tiny rug that imitates the floor pattern is a fun and practical gesture.*

Contemporary and traditional elements come together in an eclectic fashion in this free-spirited European-style bath. Quick to use what they have, Europeans have always had a flair for combining old and new treasures to produce what is often labeled a transitional look. The claw-foot tub is a classic fixture that's provided generations of bathers with satisfaction. Tiles are ancient but also very up to date, and they are as popular today as they were with the Romans. An inspired application here places a tile mosaic on the front of the vanity. The light that arcs above the sink is a modern note to jibe with the antique gold mirror. Elegant in its simplicity, this bath has few decorations. The deep saturated colors and one or two gestures—a clutch of fresh flowers on the sink, a Mediterranean blue vase no bigger than a bar of soap near the tub—proffer a design sensitivity that spells quiet luxury.

A careful choreography of color and sparkly glass lends a West Coast bath a light-filled and spacious air. Monochromatic walls expand the perimeters, while blonde wood cabinetry provides storage for any number of sundries, keeping the room neat at all times. In such tight spaces, textures and tone assume more importance and become a special design challenge. The earth-toned tiles—reminiscent of colors in the surrounding landscape—link the room to its setting and do their part to make the bath visually appear larger, too. Continuing the flooring material into the shower area without a break is a well-known technique designers often use to create a feeling of greater space. Atop the cement counter, a pair of vessel sinks add some light of their own. And although not secluded, the toilet area assumes privacy by being shielded in its own niche. In the end, the effect is clean, open, and easy to maintain.

Right: *Stacked with candles and flowers, a chic glass-and-metal console softens the minimal decor. Where windows are at a minimum, glass surfaces reflect light and keep a room from appearing gloomy.*

Opposite: *A frameless, clear-glass shower enclosure is another designer trick for making a bath appear larger than it actually is. Dual showerheads help fashion a shower that's user-friendly for two.*

Designer: Ursula E. Kloeters, ASID/Square One Interiors

No bright yellow rubber duckies lined up in this elegant bath. Instead, there are fixtures and materials that maintain the original flavor of the home. Built in 1894, the old Victorian Shingle-style house was recently revamped from top to bottom without sacrificing any of its charm. The custom-designed stained-glass windows and the light fixtures above the vanity in the new master suite addition, for example, are both in sync with the structure's age. The durable tiled floor also helps create the right tone. To facilitate a harried couple, there are dual sinks and a separate shower enclosure, both modern amenities that are very popular today. But the design is so well handled, nothing appears too glaringly new. To change the room's mood according to the season, the owners can simply switch towel colors. The neutral palette will accommodate a large variety of color choices as well as bright patterns.

Opposite: *The simple design of the vanity facilitates grooming while maintaining the character of the era in which the original house was built. A small vintagelike window on the far wall allows natural light an easy entry.* Right: *Stained glass never loses its appeal. Included in the large window next to the tub, the decorative glass enhances the bathing area. In a different situation where privacy might be an issue, colorful stained glass is often a valuable solution.*

Designer: Rick Proppe

Modern yet classic, can that be? Absolutely, and this lavish but clean-lined bath is proof of how well the styles can coexist. If you have been craving a bath that would offer all the amenities without fanfare, study this understated design for inspiration. On the contemporary side? Minimal window shades on simple windows, gleaming surfaces, and a meeting of colors pulled from nature, hues that evoke thoughts of water and sky. Note the shape of the chrome hardware glinting in the light and the lineup of complementary glass shelves that add a new edge. But also look at the abundance of traditional-style cabinetry that aids the elegant scene by keeping it always clutter-free. It's a fine marriage of elements. Yet, even so, your attention zeroes in on the whirlpool tub. Promising restoration and relaxation, the deep tub is the dramatic centerpiece that anchors this inviting room.

Above: Pulling the tub away from the wall, the owners focused on creating a more indulgent, spalike ambience. The storage adjoining the tub lends the fixture additional importance while also making way for towels, toiletries, and scented candles. Opposite: The high ceiling and undressed windows play to the room's clean, modern side. Contrasted with the dark floor, walls and cabinetry gleam, giving the room a polished attitude.

Some things never go out of style. Pearls and simple black cocktail dresses are just two examples. In the world of design, octagonal floor tiles, white beadboard, and sparkling white tile are classic. No matter how they're used, they give a setting a sense of graciousness. In these two homes, such ingredients make the difference. One uses wheat-colored tiles as accents to render its tiled walls more exciting. The other recruits a modern glass shower enclosure to update the old recipe. In this latter one, dark-wood-framed mirrors mimic the base of the soaking tub and help tie both ends of the room together. Still, neither bath is flashy with colors or fixtures. On the contrary, it's the serene-colored walls and floors that capture our emotions. A bouquet of flowers or a lone silver cup is all the embellishing either requires to be perfect.

Left: *White tile has long been a favorite for its clean, fresh appearance as well as its reflective quality. Here, a series of thoughtful details— from the glass knob on the medicine cabinet to the glass shelf—also capture the light and add sparkle.*

Opposite: *The soaking tub claims a window-side site to make the most of the water views. Located mid-center, the glassed-in shower separates the bathing area from the grooming stations. Thin marble shelves above the sinks have a distinct old-world flavor that works well with the beadboard paneling.*

Architect: Dominic Mercadante

Make a Statement

Square footage may be at a minimum, but this artful room lacks little else. Traditional-style cabinetry blended with open storage results in a furniturelike vanity that takes advantage of the high ceiling without making the space feel crowded. In the same way that large-scale furniture can sometimes enhance a small room, the well-planned assembly of drawers, cubbies, and cupboards provides stylish storage. It also creates the perception that the bath is much bigger than it is. The oversize mirror projects an illusion of grandeur, too. Suddenly, there's architectural interest where none previously existed. To play up the vertical or horizontal lines of your bath, consider custom built-in or inexpensive, ready-to-assemble bookcases. Choreograph the cabinets or shelves to complement the shape and design of your sink or tub. A smart layout of fixtures and furniture will help a bath—or any room—live up to its potential.

Opposite: *Green plants and a garden-like lattice insert flanking the tub play to the bath's fresh, airy tone. The deftly constructed vanity includes plain wooden knobs as well as small drawers with finger pulls. The vanity's two-color scheme mimics the wallcovering.*

Right: *A pale-blue-and-white color combination helps to make this small bath charming. The stripes enhance the height of the walls by leading your eye up to the ceiling. Stripes are also neat- and tailored-looking, a fine choice for tight quarters.*

Above: *Dainty blue shades on white sconces add an extra little splash of color. The simple cabinetry, pristine tile backsplash, and white mirror take on an elevated tone partnered with the dazzling yellow walls.*

Designer: Ann M. Morris, CKD/CBD

Neutrals are lovely in a bedroom or a bath, and they are also a safe route. For a real rush of summerlike zest, only intense, fearless color will do. This sprightly bath pairs sharp white woodwork and tile with citrus, wake-up yellow. It's a dynamite combination that can raise or rejuvenate standard white fixtures to new heights of interest in a flash. Classic black-and-white tiled floors, decorators know, always respond well to zingy colors like yellow, orange, sunny coral, and lime-green, particularly when there's a good dose of white involved. Of course, a lot of this fresh-looking bath's appeal is also derived from its surplus of art. A large school of fish is fun to view and extremely decorative. Framed botanicals would also be effective. But fish—because they relate to water—are a far more appropriate catch for this sunny retreat.

Left: *No everyday, shy, vanilla-colored towels here. Instead, the owners mix it up with red, yellow, and orange to complement the fish. Accents of red raise the heat and brighten the mood.*

Productive Home Offices

Since productivity requires efficiency and organization, home offices should be well-lit; should facilitate the use of computers, faxes, and printing machines; should be stocked with storage; and should be comfortable. Use the volume of work you handle to help calculate how complex a room you need.

An antique table beside a bedroom window will provide a part-time office. Dress it up with pretty pencil and writing paper holders that match the drapes or pillows. Office armoires are another simple solution. Available in styles ranging from classic to Far Eastern, these helpers combine convenience and function. Most feature a keyboard shelf, file drawers, and adjustable shelving. When your tasks are completed, close the doors and the muss disappears.

Wall-mounted shelves holding art objects and photographs help soften the "office" look, while a series of pieces in the same style and finish such as birch veneer afford a more regimented, corporate look. Happily, many of today's furnishings have casters for mobility: Roll your desk beside the window when the

roses are blooming, and move it closer toward the fire

in winter.

Rooms that spend a great deal of time empty, such

as dining rooms, make natural offices. Claim the table

as work central. When guests are due, tuck paperwork

and files in baskets, in a closet, or behind cabinet

doors. Designating one wall to hold gear frees up the

rest of the space for other furnishings like chairs and a table for late-night dinners.

Window treatments can be wood shutters,

mini-blinds, fabric shades, or drapes. Start a

collection according to your theme, and use

posters, mechanical drawings, or prints of your

interests to decorate the walls. Because you're

the boss, your office can have any combination

of intriguing materials, furnishings, and colors.

Lovable Libraries

Above: *The room's formal fireplace with splendid architectural detailing and the very traditional cabinetry underline that this is no ordinary home office. Behind the paneled doors, electronics stay out of sight. Two sets of French doors allow natural light in and form a suitable entrance and exit.*

Designer: Knudsen Woodworking; Manufacturer: Knudsen Woodworking and Comprehensive Design Services

The combination of books and paperwork is age-old. Combining a library with a home office, then, results in a work space that is conducive to thought and study. Floor-to-ceiling shelves afford easy access to books as they are needed and create an inviting reading-room air. Where space allows, comfortable chairs and sofas also promote this idea. With the addition of such furnishings, the role of the room is expanded, too. What a wonderful space for a committee meeting, a sophisticated cocktail party, or a beautifully decorated Christmas tree! Add handsome wood paneling and crown moldings to lend the library/office more architectural interest. And to enrich the traditional motif, import an antique or reproduction desk that's big enough on top to accommodate papers, phone, and family photographs and with deep drawers for hiding messier papers. With sumptuous Oriental carpets below and brass chandeliers glowing above, work hours will never seem too long.

Right: *Hardwood floors and leather upholstery are not unusual in a library/office. Nor are personal favorites such as a unique sculpture. Due to its size, this room allows space for a desk at either end so two people can work undisturbed at the same time.*

Corner Warmer

Good work! This office is so cleverly designed there's even room left over for a very welcoming sitting area by the fireplace. By placing the kidney-bean-shaped desk in the corner, the owner gained light and views. The soffit that graces the rest of the room stops here so a person at the desk never feels boxed in. With lots of vertical wall space at their disposal, framed diplomas and favorite pictures can be easily put on display. There's also a spot for a bulletin board, an every office must-have. The combination of white walls and pale wood, including the refinished plank floor, helps make the office homey. Since nothing jumps out here—no vibrant colors or patterns—the atmosphere seems tranquil. Files and books are sequestered in the antique pine trunk that also serves as a coffee table. And don't overlook the extras: A straw wastebasket, for instance, contrasts with a metal desk.

Left: *Inexpensive office furniture—especially when it comes with whimsical punch-outs—can look extraordinarily good in the right setting. Increase its modern allure with a metal file holder plus a metal cart for holding the paper overflow.*

Right: *The shiny fireplace adds panache and keeps the office snug during the winter. The safety barrier of white stones separating the heating element from the wood floor is innovative and appealing. Carved shore birds seem at home perched on the rocks! The futon is a sleep-over solution for guests.*

Above: *The curved arms on the chairs mimic the curve of the cabinets and the desk, and this translates to greater harmony in a small space. The rug echoes the room's colors. The smart layout allows the person working to shift from one work area to the next by simply moving his or her chair.*

Above: *A comfortable leather club chair welcomes visitors and affords a place for reading. Built-in drawers are stocked with office supplies. The screen—which disguises an unused door—helps balance the setting and provides another focal point.*

Custom cabinetry has transformed this home office into a slick and functional work space. The owner can schedule a meeting with clients here and be assured they'll feel like they're in good hands. A simple palette and modern furnishings supply a look that is very much in tune with the times. Electronics, papers, and reference books disappear behind doors or in drawers leaving the scene well organized. In addition to the computer table, there's a large desk—with a pleasing organic form—for spreading out plans or briefs. Light fixtures have been carefully selected for their tone as well as their function. And a few pieces of art lend a personal note without clutter. But since every successful room should also contain a surprise, there's a decorative folding screen and a reproduction antique fan. Both these choices are in step with the decor, and they're upbeat, which keeps the work humming along.

Right: *Deep drawers with curved metal pulls are compartmentalized to hold files. The interesting artwork and sculptures are personal additions. Out of the way, these decorative objects contribute a stylish note without interfering with daily transactions. The woven boxes contain extras like string and tape for mailing packages.*

Designer: Melissa Kradas; Manufacturer: Personal Style

Mission-style furniture implies a straightforward, businesslike approach in this home office. The furniture's clean lines, lack of ornamentation, and ample storage options further a sense of orderliness. With everything in its place as it should be, the owner can get down to work without rummaging through papers and clutter. Visually, the rich warm color of the oak and the rough, ruddy tones of the bricks are also pleasing. A large expanse of white wall balances the darker shades and keeps the room's overall tone welcoming and friendly. A carpet in a soft William Morris-type design interjects warmth and interest underfoot. So as not to detract from the vintage look, the owner has also opted for a complementary wood office chair rather than a sleek 21st-century design. The large window would be a gift to any setting. Plenty of natural light makes for a happier, healthier work environment.

Below: *Lead-glass doors are traditional in such settings. Pretty and practical, the glass keeps books dust-free. To complement the richly colored wood of the chairs, a fabric with a muted pattern was an appropriate selection for the chair.*

Opposite: *The handsome shade on the desk lamp is reminiscent of the leaded-artglass fixtures designed by Tiffany in the early 1900s. Decorative shades were essential elements in Arts and Crafts-style homes. The Gustav Stickley-like desk hides a pullout keyboard tray.*

Manufacturer: Thomasville Furniture

Office Essentials

Work habits vary widely. Where some prefer a cozy librarylike atmosphere, others require plentiful light and views to feel energized and creative. This office/study falls into the latter category. Lined with windows and painted in seashorelike hues, it's a space designed to allow the imagination plenty of leeway. Beadboard paneling comes across as blue as the ocean when it's teamed with snowy white woodwork. A painted floor such as this is soft in tone. Modern furnishings would work in such a sunny, open space. But to maintain the vintage tone the architecture provokes, the owners wisely opted for furnishings that speak to the past. The high-legged desk with its drop-down front also delivers options. When the owner is sketching, the slanted top can act as a work surface; letter-writing and reading are more comfortable using the flat interior area. A stool—at just the right height—accommodates both activities.

Above: *Too often nooks and crannies that could serve as display areas are overlooked. Here, the owner makes unconventional use of a window to show off a favorite painting. Not all work rooms have to be sterile. Surround yourself with personal mementos, flowers, and art to stir the creative juices.*

Manufacturer: Thomasville Furniture

Left: *Move furnishings away from the wall, and let them shine! Textures—the green plant, the sisal carpet, the Asian-inspired baskets, even the starfish above the windows—give this sunny atelier its verve. A narrow, freestanding bookshelf makes way for an additional tide of treasures without demanding too much square footage.*

Home Advantage

Removed from the world of stereotypes, the best home offices are high on personality, and yours should be too. Whether you're a full-time nine-to-fiver or a part-time worker, the requisites for a home office remain identical. The ambience, however, can be whatever you desire. Here one work space exudes a modern flavor. The other, with a wood countertop and antique chair, comes across as traditional. Still, look how much they share in common. Their straightforward design includes abundant natural light to make hours at the desk less stressful, bountiful storage to facilitate everything from paying bills to compiling reports, and a practical layout. With everything right at hand, there's no need to waste energy running for the phone or searching for items. Bright white walls and ceilings also play an important role, fostering a clean, no-fuss, no-frill air for those who want to concentrate.

Left: *Designating one wall for storage not only makes the room more interesting but also solves the storage dilemma. The owners included simple shades to diffuse the light, a soft patterned rug, and a small sofa to create a friendlier environment for meetings.* **Architect: John Gillespie**

Right: *This generous work area has it all, from pullout keyboard tray to tons of countertop room. To tie in with the beadboard paneling, the owners stash little supplies in Shaker boxes. Glass-fronted upper cabinets hold pretty glasses and dishes, while open shelves are set aside for books.*

Desk Jobs

The most advanced computers don't require contemporary stations. All sorts of options exist for setting up a home office from lovely antique or reproduction desks to slabs of wood set upon rustic sawhorse legs. If your style is traditional, you won't be comfortable laboring away in a cube-like environment with a cold metal table. Arrange your home office—or the section of a room you've designated as your part-time work space—to reflect your taste. These two elegant work spots can serve as guides. In each, the desk is the highlight. If there are files and paperwork, it's all neatly and secretly contained in desk drawers or nearby cabinetry so the scene remains orderly. A messy accumulation of books and mail could quickly hamper productivity not to mention hurt the ambience. Each also has adequate light, a comfortable chair, and one or two personal touches that speak to the owner's heart.

Left: *A drop-front antique desk befits the spirit of an older home with wide board floors and wood beams. The sloping ceiling cozies up the area, affording it a more intimate tone. Barn-red (an exclamation point of color) woodwork is traditional in Colonial homes.* **Architects: Centerbrook Architects**

Left: *One corner of this gracious room has been given over to work. The owner has arranged it, though, so outdoor views can be relished while the matters at hand are dealt with. Decorative brass rods mimic the tone of the desk's hardware and afford the sophisticated drapes additional glamour.*

Luxury in today's frantic world? A quiet study set aside from the rest of the house where it's possible to claim a few moments for writing notes or reading the paper? Not as implausible as it sounds, such a space can also be a multipurpose room used as a home office or a part-time guest room. Create one for yourself that's as pretty as this with a serene palette and versatile furnishings. For instance, choose a sleeper sofa and a secretary that will also hide a computer or a television. Window seats, big or small, are a no-fail way to forge extra storage and seating. If there's a fireplace, no other focal point is needed. If not, create a visual centerpiece with a useful armoire or a large oil painting. This is a decidedly feminine room, but neither gender would turn down an opportunity to spend an afternoon here with a favorite novel.

Left: *Mixing muted greens and soft pinks is a soothing recipe for a small room dedicated to quiet times. The patterns share the same cool color range and so work well together. Pots of trailing ivy soften the marble mantel. The dainty tray-style table is a delicate substitute for a coffee table.*

Left: *Fabric-covered
walls sport a quartet of
bewitching bird prints.
The prints' stylized
backdrop is similar to
the decorative paint-
ing found on the
secretary. Many
designers advise a spot
of black in every room
for elegance, thus, the
smart lamp shade.*

**Designer: Decor of
Greenwich, Inc.**

Doing It Your Way

An office that will keep the tools of your trade, your papers, or craft projects accessible and tidy takes planning. Many different styles of desks, modulars, and office armoires are available. Browse design magazines and catalogs to find furnishings that will make the most of your space while also complementing your home. For a rustic European demeanor, for example, consider a desk that includes a hutch. Finished in white, a piece like this would enhance a Swedish-inspired room. In natural pine, the hutch would bring additional charm to an English or French country decor. A sawhorse desk claims less space and provides storage. Move in some portable wall shelves, and fashion a configuration that's suitable for your room's design. Tall open shelves make the most of wall space. To prevent your new shelves from appearing jumbled, gather baskets and stackable boxes to hide smaller items.

Above: *Built-in attractions like storage drawers and a file drawer make this desk with hutch unit an office unto itself. Given center stage or snuggled into a corner, it's sure to upgrade an everyday ho-hum space. For an eclectic look that doesn't scream "office," team the desk with a nontraditional office chair.*

Right: *Flexible furnishings have a number of advantages. Open shelves against the wall and on this desk, for instance, hold supplies. They also showcase pretty flowers and personal touches. Delineate your work space from the rest of the room with an area rug.*

Retailer: Ballard Designs

A foyer is where guests pause to shed coats or park briefcases; hallways are your routes to here and there; landings are where you stop to catch your breath. Mudrooms, laundry rooms, attics—all these unappreciated spaces have a role. With a little creativity, you can make them charming and functional.

Sometimes referred to as a vestibule or entrance hall, a foyer should be a preview of what's ahead—in color and style. If the rest of your house is formal, for instance, a chandelier would be an inkling as to the gracious living room that follows. If you're the casual type, skip crystal and think black iron. Light neutral colors expand small foyers; uplifting

colors like lemon-yellow or orange will make them cheerful; rich dark shades such as burgundy or chocolate lend an elegant tone.

Marble, tile, or slate? If it's a small entry, go ahead and splurge on the floor. For a larger area, whether the mood is dressy or relaxed, black-and-white vinyl squares have a timeless appeal. Paint is another alternative. How about a stenciled or trompe l'oeil design? To protect wall-to-wall carpeting, lay down a colorful kilim or rag rug.

A roomy closet is invaluable. But an entryway bench that provides a place to sit, a lid that lifts for storing boots, and hooks for hanging coats is also a utilitarian addition. A bench painted snowy white with a tall beadboard-paneled back would fit a clean-lined country home. For a period look, antique Victorian hat stands, also with hooks attached and a mirror, often turn up at antique shops and auctions. Mirrors increase the sense of light and allow people to adjust their caps or hair as they enter and exit. Is there room for an armoire? Fitted with hooks and a shelf, armoires are catchalls for everything from jackets to golf clubs. A stand made of iron, wood, or metal or a large ceramic pot for umbrellas and walking sticks is picturesque and handy.

The most common solution for breathing life into a hall is to treat it as a gallery. In a uniform fashion, hang prints, photographs, or botanical drawings. For cohesion, keep the framing treatments similar in style and look: black frames, say, or gold. If there's a jig in the hall's shape, a little

shelf, mounted on the wall with brackets (slide a stool underneath), and a light will create an intimate place to pen a note or make a call without impinging on floor space. Wall-to-ceiling shelves filled with books (an 8-inch depth for most volumes) add a cozy library touch. And a hall or stair landing with a window and a window seat is everyone's favorite.

If neither windows nor skylights are feasible, install adequate lighting and use color to generate a feeling of light. Pale halls, though, can sometimes look drab. Jewel tones

and rich designerlike colors—crimson, deep peach, sun-baked terra-cotta—spell instant glamour.

To organize the paraphernalia that collects in a mudroom, look to plastic bins in wild colors, baskets, or something unpredictable like canvas bags. Generous built-in cubbies will also keep things neat and visible. Stencil a family member's name above each slot, or have the bags monogrammed.

A portable gardening bench stationed in the corner will afford a green-thumbed gardener a place to pot bulbs or arrange flowers. And a deep laundry sink will make washing a large pot or pet less of a chore.

Floor and wall treatments in the mudroom need to be long-wearing. Consider alkyd paints and scrubbable wallcoverings along with materials like stone, vinyl, and linoleum. Like any other room in the house, a mudroom gains personality when you add window treatments and art.

Laundry rooms also welcome pretty papers and bright paint. Stepping out of their drudge roles, the best ones boast cabinetry and counters for folding and stacking. Clever extras—built-in ironing boards, fold-down sewing tables—make these spaces multifunctional. If possible, plug in a window for natural light and give it a tailored shade or a pert curtain.

With skylights or dormers to let in light and air, a lowly attic is transformed. Rather than battle with the quirky angled ceilings, use them to forge unique, personality-filled rooms. Station shorter furnishings to take advantage of the tight space under the eaves and move larger pieces like beds or sofas toward the room's middle. Attics are made for built-ins. Line the walls with bookshelves for a cozy look or light-toned cabinetry for a modern take. A wall of bookshelves or folding screens across one end visually shortens a long room. Let your imagination take wing—up this high, anything goes.

Every home benefits from a mudroom. These are the blessed spaces where you can kick off the wet shoes, the snowy coats, or the garden clogs. Seemingly oblivious to water and dirt, the very best mudrooms have tile or stone floors that can be easily washed up and deep laundry sinks that can be used for laundry, for potting plants, or for washing the family pet! To render yours as useful as these, install hooks for hanging coats or baskets, a wood box or barrel for holding firewood (it will save you a trip through the dark to the wood pile), and a rack for drying mittens or kitchen curtains or whatever it is that needs drying. The decoration should tie in with the style of your home but can be as simple as pale walls and bare windows. Interestingly enough, the friendly, eclectic flotsam and jetsam that accumulate will give the space personality.

Right: *A collection of skis, a mass of wood, and a fine drying rack for bottles make an alluring vignette. Even the old cutting board leaning against the wall has sculptural magic. Organize what you need in baskets of varying sizes to achieve a farmhouse mood.*

Opposite: *A red tile floor is a good choice for a mudroom that doesn't shy away from water. Attractive blue-and-white-striped curtains make this sunny space charming. Line up the family's boots, and add a flower, and you will have created a very country look.*

Left: *Pale walls and a mirror enhance the effects of a trompe l'oeil mural that depicts a green, open space. Without the swirling sky presented on the ceiling, the mural—and the mood—would be incomplete.*

Awkwardly shaped hallways often present a problem. They can be dark and uninteresting, too thin and long, or all of the above. Decorative paint—especially techniques such as trompe l'oeil—can turn all that around. Translated from the French, trompe l'oeil means "trick the eye," and that's just what an artist does when a three-dimensional space on a flat surface is created. This fabulous hall was once a misfit but no longer. A cloud-swept ceiling and a stone arch beckon visitors to enter a world of fantasy. With a new perspective of green grass stretching into the distance and sky above, the previously cramped interior feels opened with color and light. You can forget you're inside and give your-self over to daydreams of long summer walks and flowers. If you're worried about the cost of hiring a professional artist, consider tracking down an art student or choosing a pictorial wallcovering.

Right: *Before, there was no light. Now, visitors pause at the wooden bench to soak up the illusion of bringing the outdoors in. The mono-chromatic floor and walls are a fine segue for the natural tones of the mural.*

Designer: Anjum Razvi, ASID

Think how many times you use the hall—up and down, back and forth. Why not make every trip a pleasure? This home's Southwestern architecture provides for stucco walls, a beamed ceiling, and a brick floor every bit as enticing as the yellow brick road. Bright woven rugs mark the way. There are niches for romantic candles as well as more practical overhead lights. And there are windows and French doors so travelers catch views along the way. One window with a particularly fine vista has a bench nearby. The bench is an invitation to sit and rejuvenate for a few minutes by soaking up the scenery. Perhaps, you have a window in your hall where you can set a little stool or a rocker? A builder could plug in a small window and transform your once gloomy hall into a place where you'll want to linger.

Opposite: *As warm and cozy as the adjoining living room, this hall offers a sitting place, windows, and ambience. The brick floor is durable and attractive. At night with candles glowing, the red bricks blaze with color.*

Right: *During daylight hours, the same hall is flooded with light. The creamy-colored stucco complements the brick floor but also prevents the narrow space from feeling too cramped. The woven rugs duplicate the red and beige color scheme.*

Architect: Bennett Wagner Grody; Designer: In-Site Design Group

A Grand Entrance

Above: *The length of the hall allows room for several seating groups. Nestled beside the stairs, twin chairs and a handsome antique chest invite company. What a fine place to read the newspaper! Adhering to a similar palette in the hall as well as up the stairs helps link the spaces together.*

Above: *The curve of the second-floor landing and stair rail creates a natural site for two chairs and a table. The lamp makes the arrangement useful rather than merely pretty. Photographs and trophies stored behind glass will remain protected from dust and fingerprints.*

Too often taken for granted, entries and hallways go unnoticed and unused. To make the most of the square footage such spaces provide, study the possibilities. According to the architecture, select a mood that is formal or relaxed. A library table, a lamp to provide a soft glow, and a comfortable chair or two can forge a spot for relaxing or for looking over the daily mail. A pair of inviting armchairs—with a round table in between—becomes a meeting site for conversation or a cup of afternoon tea. Cushy rugs—and don't forget stair runners—can help lay a foundation for colors and accessories like light fixtures and green plants. Rather than display family memorabilia on open shelves where dust collects, consider bookshelves with glass doors. Once in place and in use, you'll wonder how you did without these surprise settings before.

Right: *A remarkable foyer deserves royal treatment. Relying on a palette of greens, golds, and rose, combined with a cognac hue evident in the marble floors, the designers chose damask drapes, pendant chandeliers, and a hand-woven wool rug. Green plants soften the mood and make the space more user-friendly.*

Designer: Jane Bade, ASID, and Joy Wolfe, ASID

Laundry. The very word is enough to instill dread or, at least, it used to be. Not so long ago, a laundry room might have meant the dreary corner of a basement or a windowless closet. Happily, we've seen the last of those days. Modern laundry rooms welcome all kinds of interpretations. One currently popular style calls for light-colored walls, cheerful wallcoverings, and long-wearing wood floors like those found in these rooms. Ideally, to handle the amount of sorting, stacking, and folding that will transpire, there should also be a table or a counter. If possible, create a space that will allow you to set up the ironing board. Since you want every room where you spend time to be welcoming, give your laundry room a special face. Recruit baskets or glass jars to hold supplies, add a plant, and hang a pert curtain at the window.

Left: *White prevails in this sweet room along with the whimsical paper. As a safety feature, the lofty shelf is at the right height for parents but too high for little hands. Baskets are an inexpensive, foolproof way to organize.* Designer: Seabrook Designs "Cuttin' Up"

Right: *As cheerful as a button, this workday room can't help but make you smile. From the colorful border that adorns the wall to the plaid window valance, it's a scene designed to lighten the laundry-day load. The pine table serves as a counter but provides an airier look.* Designer: Seabrook Designs "Above & Beyond"

Left: *The contrast of oak floor and white cabinetry is simple and striking. Shaker-style storage maximizes leftover space beneath the stairs and also provides a display area. A neutral-colored stair runner is a good choice for the low-key scene.*

Creativity counts. The more you study your home—each little nook and cranny—the more apt you are to discover pockets of wasted space. Take time to consider how you can utilize these neglected niches to enhance your lifestyle. A typical under-the-stairs wedge of square footage like the one pictured here could have gone overlooked. Instead with some careful planning, it's become a convenient work area. Important notices, appointment dates, and emergency numbers are posted on the handy bulletin board. Nearby, a set of built-in Shaker-style drawers hold necessary items like phone books and paper. Because the desk is centrally located, mom or dad can work here and still keep track of the comings and goings of family members. If the pressure of bill-paying and schedule-juggling grows too tiresome, the whimsical tin figures posted aloft on the outside wall will pick up the owners' flagging spirits in no time.

Opposite: *Flanking the work area, a precious sliver of shelving is an ideal place to show off favorite pieces that may go unnoticed elsewhere. The golden tones of the wicker and wood ladder-back chair against the white desk repeat the color scheme of the adjoining staircase.*

Architects: Andrew Chary & Associates

Left: *Tucked in the corner, the sink is a boon to all. Metal towel bars installed above allow people to grab a towel as needed. Under the sink, there are shelves for supplies as well as assorted toiletries like hand soap and lotion. Wall-mounted cabinets, painted a yellow shade, also provide storage.*

A room that serves as entry, mudroom, and laundry room should be designed to take a lot of abuse, since fingerprints and wet feet are a matter of course. And coats and hats appear and disappear like so many leaves in a windstorm. The solutions: Rugged wood paneling that won't show every smudge, and plenty of storage. That doesn't mean forsaking wallpaper or decorative paint. On the contrary, this room combines some William Morris-like wallpaper with its paneling. The combination of the honey color of the wood and the red, green, gold, and blue of the paper elevates the room to something more than just a work space.

Sure, the sink is here for washing up, and there are a washer and dryer, too. But there's also a handsome tack-room quality that presents the room with a gracious country air. To further that feeling, horse bridles and halters are welcome.

Left: *An upholstered seat allows people a place to sit while changing shoes or removing riding boots. Iron pegs are sturdy holders for the ever-changing roster of outdoor gear. Horse pictures add to the equestrian ambience.*

Designer: Trisha Reger/Reger Designs

A contemporary house has been made more efficient with the addition of an entry that includes a roomy closet, a powder room, and a pantry. So as not to distract from the rest of the house, these spaces employ colors and materials found in the other rooms. The soft neutral walls are painted with scrubbable paint, and the tiled floor requires only a quick mop when the kids run in with muddy feet. A straightforward built-in bench with a wainscoted front is a dual-purpose element serving as a shelf for boots or as a seat. To augment the closet, there are also coat hooks mounted on the wall and a shelf to keep hats that don't lend themselves to squishing safely out of the way. A display shelf, a primitive painting, and a pretty plate interject color and let it be known that even a functional space can be stylish.

Opposite: *A collection of* The New Yorker *magazine covers fashions a creative wallcovering for the powder room. Teamed with bright white wainscoting, the effect is clever and clean. Fun additions like the key holder mounted on the wall help keep family members organized.*

Left: *Positioned near the entry and the kitchen, the sunny pantry makes putting away the groceries a snap. A second fridge located here creates space for soda and bottled water. Brass hardware catches the light and also lends cohesion to the rooms.*

Left: *A set of skylights floods the attic space with sunlight giving it tree house charm. Sisal carpeting atop a wood floor is a clean look. The bright blue open bookcase tucked along the wall provides plentiful storage without fighting with the room's sloping ceiling.* Right: *In addition to the sky-light, the owners punched a fixed window at the end of their bonus room for added light and views. A judicious use of white and deep blue accentuates the attic's interesting shape. Wall-to-wall carpeting equals less noise and completes the picture.*

Manufacturer: Velux America Inc.

Too often, admit it, your needs have to take a backseat. These owners knew what they wanted and pursued their dreams. One coveted an office with a drawing board to allow her space to work on her designs at home. The other envisioned a room where he could spend a few hours exercising before and after work. With a little ingenuity, they each got what they hoped. Forget adding on; unused attic space yielded a perfect spot for the architect and the health-watcher. Today, skylights—without the expense of constructing dormers—let in the air and the light. If you haven't explored the possibility of transforming your forlorn attic, now is the time. A guest room, a teen's private hideaway, a quiet sitting spot for you and your spouse to relax? With new finished walls and floors, previously dilapidated attics can give even a small house grand possibilities.

According to feng shui experts, an entry—the first room visitors see—has the power to influence the flow of energy through an entire home. You want yours to be clutter free, bright, practical, and welcoming—just like this space. A tiled floor is an ideal surface for shoes that are sometimes wet. And light walls or wallcoverings will draw people in. This California house has its entry on the ground floor. Floating stairs travel up to the first floor, which houses the living room, dining room, kitchen, and master bedroom suite. Because it's a well-used route, the entry is a perfect show-off spot for family heirlooms or special treasures. A grandfather clock, for instance, marks the time. And an impressive commode provides storage for mittens, hats, or extra sweaters. Entries and hallways needn't be dull. Draw inspiration from this formal portal, and dress yours with collectibles, art, or faux painting.

Opposite: *Fully carpeted treads give a new look to contemporary floating stairs. To personalize the space and also as an introduction to the home's style, the owners incorporated an upholstered chair and a set of antique prints along with a handsome grandfather clock.*

Left: *Whatever your entry's size, add color and texture with a tabletop display. A bouquet of fresh flowers or a green plant will give the space warmth. Here, neutral-colored paneling dramatizes the gold-leafed mirror and wall brackets. Try an Asian or a decoratively painted table, too, and see the difference!*

Designer: Joseph P. Horan, FASID

If only every home could have a functional, handsome space such as this! Rain or shine, a mudroom designed with a durable stone, tile, or vinyl floor never lets you down. This one has a surplus amount of charm thanks to the antique nature of its beamed ceiling and the plethora of open shelves. Lined with jars of homemade preserves and canned vegetables fresh from the garden, the small space presents a welcoming face to each and every visitor. Bunches of hanging dried herbs and flowers along with some baskets also lend a country, come-into-our-home air. Kids pause only long enough to drop their baseball bat or hockey stick, kick off their shoes, and then they're gone. Still, if muddy hands need a wash or flowers need water, the sink stands ready. In fact, the cook could use this sunswept sink when the peas need shelling or the beans snapping.

Opposite: *The rustic stone floor in this English-flavored space adds to the room's character. Paneled walls are durable and forgiving. For storage, the owners turn to barrels and shelves.*

Right: *Auxiliary spaces provide storage for an overflow of cookware, books, and supplies. A simple stool placed sink-side affords a gardener a place to sit while arranging flowers. The wee window above the sink pulls in additional light and also allows a different view of the outdoors.*

A modern house requires a laundry room with an edgy appeal. The formula for getting chores done doesn't change, but the look can. Forge a room that's streamlined, one that emphasizes form and function as the two pictured here do. White walls, simple storage, and slick surfaces are key. Some families prefer storage that allows them to see what they have or need in a hurry. Tidy piles of soap and linens have a visual appeal that can also enhance the design in much the same way that stacks of tableware and copper pots will in a kitchen. Others want all the goods hidden neatly behind closed doors. Whatever you decide, for practicality's sake, it's wise to install a rack where items can be hung after they are ironed or while they dry. And appointing each family member a separate bin or basket saves sorting time on items like socks—those runaways that defy matching!

Right: *Plastic has its place in the laundry room. Collect bins in various colors for easy identification. A built-in counter becomes a center for crafts and sewing as well as sorting. Surprise! The miniature door in the wall hides a drop-down ironing board.*

Right: *Resist the urge to add a mishmash of elements; stick to what you need. A sink is always a treasure for soaking delicate garments or washing hands. An adjustable shelving unit is a thrifty and futuristic-looking storage solution.* **Architects: Elliot & Elliot Architects**

This spacious 1920s house had something to offer that long went unrecognized. A renovation finally brought the overlooked attic's potential to light, and—as they say—the rest is history. Where once there was unused space now exists a spectacular and private master suite. The heavenly retreat includes a bedroom and bath as well as a living/entertainment room for the owners. A series of new skylights pull in the sun and light up what used to be a dark and gloomy space. To maximize the fresh, airy, up-and-away feeling, the walls are painted a crisp white and furnishings are minimal. A pale wall-to-wall carpet pulls it all together and muffles noise at the same time. And a plentiful amount of built-in storage maintains order. An architect or a space-planner can help you stake claim to an unused attic, basement, or garage, too. Call in an expert, and watch the possibilities unfold.

Left: *Sliding the pedestal sink into its own niche saves space in the narrow bath and imbues the fixture with more presence. With proper lighting to the left and right and handy towel racks at your fingertips on either side, the area becomes a well-organized grooming station. New skylights provide greater daytime visibility.*
Right: *An Arts and Crafts-style fixture illuminates the living/entertainment area. Thanks to the attic's sloping walls, nooks, and crannies, the unit has a good deal of built-in visual interest and coziness. Tucked-away bookshelves do their job without intruding on the compact room.*

**Architect: Thom Greene;
Designer: Rick Proppe**

Resource Directory

ARCHITECTS

Andrew Chary & Associates
460 Old Post Rd.
Old Bedford, NY 10506
phone 914-234-6289
(296–297, 300–301)

Bennett Wagner Grody
1123 Auraria Parkway
Denver, CO 80401
phone 303-623-7323
fax 303-623-2836
(85, 94–95, 290–291)

Hank Bruce, A/A
23 B Main St.
Tiburon, CA 94920
phone 415-435-9118
(242–243)

Burt & Weinrich Architects
P.O. Box 1389
Damariscotta, ME 04543
phone 207-563-3911
(110–111)

Centerbrook Architects
67 Main St.
Centerbrook, CT 06409
phone 860-767-0175
(276)

Clark Robins Design/Build. Inc.
3333 Pinebrook Dr.
Richmond, VA 23225
phone 804-330-0193
fax 804-330-0195
(28)

Evan Eglin
7840 E. Broadway Blvd.
Tucson, AZ 85710
phone 520-886-5770
(54)

Elliot & Elliot Architects
P.O. Box 318
Blue Hill, ME 04614
phone 207-374-2566
(308)

David Estreich
David Estreich Architects
149 Fifth Ave.
New York, NY 10010
phone 212-475-6636
fax 212-979-0326
(63, 172, 174–175, 224–225)

John Gillespie
P.O. Box K
Camden, ME 04843
phone 207-236-8054
(274)

Frank Glynn
Stafford & Glynn Architects
425½ Main St.
El Sequndo, CA 90245
phone 310-322-0022
(71)

Thom Greene
Greene & Proppe Design, Inc.
1209 W. Berwyn Ave.
Chicago, IL 60640
phone 773-271-1925
fax 773-271-1936
info@gpdchicago.com
www.gpdchicago.com
(252–253, 285, 310–311)

Robert D. Henry
Robert D. Henry Architects
37 E. 18th St.
10th Fl.
New York, NY 10003
phone 212-533-4145
fax 212-598-9028
rdh-architects.com
(52)

Latina Homes
25300 Lorain Rd.
Ste. 3A
North Olmsted, OH 44070
phone 440-734-5100
fax 440-734-5104
lanee@latinahomes.com
www.latinahomes.com
(30)

Doug McIntosh
McIntosh/Poris
36801 Woodward
Ste. 200
Birmingham, MI 48009
phone 248-258-9346
fax 248-258-0967
mcipor@earthlink.com
(126–127)

Dominic Mercadante
70 Waldo Ave.
Belfast, ME 04915
phone 207-338-4089
(257)

Mojo Stumer Associates
14 Plaza Rd.
Greenvale, NY 11548
phone 516-625-3344
fax 516-625-3418
m.stumer@mojostumer.com
(8, 51, 84, 88–89)

Ron Robinette
3555 N. Mountain Ave.
Tucson, AZ 85719
phone 520-323-3979
(32, 176–177)

Sidnam Petrone Gartner
    Architects
136 W. 21st St.
6th Fl.
New York, NY 10011
phone 212-366-5500
fax 212-366-6559
info@spgarchitects.com
www.spgarchitects.com
(47, 90–91)

Ray Spehar
Concourse Design
17472 Ventura Blvd.
Encino, CA 91316
phone 818-995-3555
fax 818-995-4855
(84, 92–93)

Angelo Luigi Tartaglia
Via Boezio 92 D9A
Rome 00192
ITALY
phone 011-39-06-687-3879
fax 011-39-06-686-8449
tartaglia.alt@tisealinet.it
www.angeloluigitartaglia.it
(46, 62, 78, 130–131, 162–163)

Turner Lechner & Romero
435 S. Guadalupe
Santa Fe, NM 80501
phone 505-982-9469
fax 505-986-1583
(142–143)

BUILDERS

The Kemmerly Company
5235 N. Sabino Canyon Rd.
#101
Tucson, AZ 85750
phone 520-615-8900
fax 520-615-8902
chris@kemmerly.com
(54)

Old Pueblo Remodelers
1700 S. 4th Ave.
Tucson, AZ 85719
phone 520-884-8685
fax 520-629-0957
ladmin@aol.com
www.pueblo-remodel.com
(32, 176–177)

DESIGNERS

Anne Cooper Interiors, Inc.
80 Clarke Rd.
Bernardsville, NJ 07924
phone 908-696-0464
(41)

Jane Bade
Jane Bade Interiors
5575 Terrace Dr.
La Crescenta, CA 91214
(283, 292–293)

Ron Becker, ASID
Becker Interiors, Inc.
8453-I Tyco Rd.
Vienna, VA 22182
phone 703-556-9716
fax 703-556-9717
beckerinteriors@aol.com
www.beckerinteriors.com
(10)

Darla Blake, ASID, CID
Darla's Unique & Chic Interiors
10146 Riverside Dr.
Toluca Lake, CA 91602-2532
phone 818-762-2100
fax 818-762-2300
darla@uniqueandchic.com
www.uniqueandchic.com
(222–223)

Janet Brown
5 Carriage Hill Circle
Southborough, MA 01772
phone 508-485-0930
fax 508-485-7432
jbint8@aol.com
(196, 200–201, back cover)

Pamela Bytner, CKD
20 W. Washington St.
Ste. 6A
Clarkston, MI 48346
phone 248-922-0065
fax 248-922-0249
bytner@ameritech.net
www.bytnerdesign.com
(126–127)

Judy Campbell, ASID
1131 Heatherside Rd.
Pasadena, CA 91105
phone 626-796-7853
(71)

Lori Carroll, ASID, IIDA
1200 N. El Dorado Pl.
Ste. B200
Tucson, AZ 85715
phone 520-886-3443
fax 520-886-1768
lori@loricarroll.com
www.loricarroll.com
(32, 54, 176–177)

Kirsten Cavan and Anna Marie
    Madsen
Gridley Company
122 Orchard City Dr.
Campbell, CA 95008-2996
phone 408-374-0900
fax 408-374-0924
kirstenc@gridleycompany.com
www.gridleycompany.com
(72)

Sandra Elizabeth Clinger
Lifestyle Interior Design
1925 E. Fourth Pl.
Denver, CO 80206
phone 303-388-1565
fax 303-388-9067
lifestyle@ecentral.com
(38)

Christopher Coleman
70 Washington St.
Ste. 1005
Brooklyn, NY 11201
phone 718-222-8984
(108–109)

Kuche Cucina/Amir Ilin
489 Rte. 17 S.
Paramus, NJ 07652
phone 201-261-5221
(164–165, back cover)

Darryl Wilson Design
8404 Hollywood Blvd.
Los Angles, CA 90069
phone 323-822-0770
(29)

Decor of Greenwich, Inc.
164 Mason St.
Greenwich, CT 06830
phone 203-869-7100
(278–279)

Drysdale & Associates Interior
    Design
1733 Connecticut Ave. N.W.
Washington, DC 20009
phone 202-588-0700
(188–189)

Eric Mitchell Shore Design
4465 Woodley Ave.
Encino, CA 91436
phone 818-986-6436
fax 818-986-6463
emsd-beverly@att.net
(84, 92–93, 96–97)

Gail Green
Green & Co.
979 Third Ave.
New York, NY 10022
phone 212-906-0110
fax 212-906-0111
gegandco@aol.com
(63, 172, 174–175, 204–205,
    224–225)

Tom Hasenfang and
    Richard F. Hendrick, CKD
Custom Kitchens, Inc.
6412 Horsepen Rd.
Richmond, VA 23226
phone 804-288-7247
fax 804-282-2479
Richard@customkitchensinc.net
Tom@customkitchensinc.net
www.customkitchensinc.net
(144–145)

Joseph P. Horan, FASID
3299 Washington St.
San Francisco, CA 94115-1601
phone 415-346-5646
fax 415-922-0719
hor347@aol.com
www.designfinder.com/Horan
(6, 69, 173, 192–193, 304–305)

In-Site Design Group
1280 S. Clayton St.
Ste. A
Denver, CO 80210
phone 303-691-9000
fax 303-691-9229
insite@insite-design-
    group.com
www.insite-design-group.com
(85, 94–95, 290–291)

Dennis Jenkins
Dennis Jenkins & Assoc.
5813 S.W. 68th St.
South Miami, FL 33143
phone 305-665-6960
fax 305-665-6971
designerman424@aol.com
(18, 210–211)

Jean Kezeor, ASID
Comprehensive Design
1040 Main St.
#207B
Napa, CA 94559
phone 707-252-0709
fax 707-252-0625
jean@compdes.biz
www.designfinder.com
(17, 242–243)

Ursula E. Kloeters, ASID
Square One Interiors
57 Lurline St.
San Francisco, CA 94122
phone 415-664-3773
fax 415-664-1657
ursula@squareoneinteriors.com
www.squareoneinteriors.com
(250–251)

Carol R. Knott
430 Green Bay Rd.
Kenilworth, IL 60043
(197, 220–221)

Knudsen Woodworking
6150 Street Rd.
Kirkwood, PA 17536
phone 717-529-4011
fax 717-529-4010
www.knudsenwoodworking.com
(264–265)

Melissa Kradas
252 Hunters Trail
Madison, CT 06443
phone 203-245-8018
(268–269)

Stacey Lapuk, ASID, CID
Stacey Lapuk Interior Design,
    Inc.
437 Wellesley Ave.
Mill Valley, CA 94941
phone 415-383-9223;
    877-725-2900
fax 415-381-6646
lapuk@pacbell.net
www.staceylapukinteriors.com
(49, 228–229)

Douglas B. Leake, CKD
6412 Horsepen Rd.
Richmond, VA 23226
phone 804-288-7247
fax 804-282-2479
doug@customkitchensinc.net
www.customkitchensinc.net
(28)

Mark Cutler Design, Inc.
8656 Holloway Plaza Dr.
West Hollywood, CA 90069
phone 310-360-6212
fax 310-360-6213
(150–151)

Michael Whaley Interiors, Inc.
2135 E. 56th St.
New York, NY 10022
(contents, 197, 216–217)

Ann M. Morris, CKD/CBD
2100 S. Ocean Dr.
Ft. Lauderdale, FL 33316
www.kitchen-design-ny.com
(232, 260–261)

Dan and Judy Mulligan
JPM Originals
P.O. Box 482
Gladstone, NJ 07934
phone 908-879-6728
(68)

Louis Nardolillo, CKD
1086 Route 58
Riverhead, NY 11901
phone 631-727-8062
(160–161)

Mark Newman
Newman Studio
1188 Sierra Way
Palm Springs, CA 92264
phone 760-778-6900
fax 760-778-6903
(134–135)

J. Mike Patrick
2811 Big Horn Ave.
Cody, WY 82414
phone 800-653-2391
fax 307-527-7409
jmike@newwest.com
www.newwest.com
(45)

David M. Plante
533 N. Huntley Dr.
West Hollywood, CA 90048
phone 310-659-5058
fax 310-659-3408
dmp@dmpid.com
www.dmpid.com
(36)

Mark Polo
Polo, M.A. Interior Design
1107 Buckingham Rd.
Fort Lee, NJ 07024
phone 201-224-0322
(116–117)

Rick Proppe
Greene & Proppe Design, Inc.
1209 W. Berwyn Ave.
Chicago, Il 60640
phone 773-271-1925
fax 773-271-1936
info@gpdchicago.com
www.gpdchicago.com
(252–253, 285, 310–311)

Allen Ransome and Randall
   Vansyock
Fly Creek, NY 13337
phone 607-547-5774
(59)

Anjum Razvi
14829 Penasquitos Court
San Diego, CA 92129
phone 858-672-8831
fax 858-672-8831
Arazvi@san.rr.com
(288–289)

Trisha Reger
Reger Designs
45 Tudor City Pl.
Ste. 611
New York, NY 10017
phone 212-557-6262
(298–299)

Adrienne Rich
A&R Interiors
26 Broadway
Denville, NJ 07834
phone 973-625-8950
(86, 102–103)

Laura Rosenberg-Moffit
Rosenberg-Moffit Interior
   Design
435 Ryder Rd.
Manhasset, NY 11030
phone 516-365-5633
(166–167)

Samuel Botero Associates, Inc.
323 E. 53rd St.
New York, NY 10022
phone 212-935-5155
(87, 118–119)

John & Melia Strittmatter
445 Main St.
Ridgefield, CT 06877
phone 203-438-7119
jstritt@aol.com
(154–155)

Susan Thorn Interior Design
88 N. Salem Rd.
Cross River, NY 10518
phone 914-763-5265
(190–191)

Sallie Trout
Trout Studios
2727 Eleventh St.
Santa Monica, CA 90405
phone 310-581-9041
fax 310-581-9030
www.troutstudios.com
(67)

Joan Viele, CKD
Kitchen Dimensions
150 S. St. Francis "C"
Santa Fe, NM 87501
phone 505-986-8820
fax 505-986-5888
kitdim@aol.com
(120, 128–129, 136–137,
   142–143)

Christina Waag
CW Design Company
122-B N. Hamilton Dr.
Beverly Hills, CA 90211
phone 310-623-4082
fax 310-623-4083
Christina@CWDesignCo.com
www.CWDesignCo.com
(51)

Kari Whitman
1155 N. La Cienega
#812
Los Angeles, CA 90069
phone 310-652-8684
fax 310-652-8688
kwinteriors@aol.com
asidla.org
(194–195)

Mary Wisman
614 W. Lamme
Bozeman, MT 59715
phone 406-587-7636
fax 406-587-7636
mwisman@mcn.net
(138–139)

Joy Wolfe
Designed with Joy Interiors
9420 Carlyn Pl.
Jujunga, CA 91042
phone 818-248-7499
(283, 292–293)

Haruko Yoshida, ASID, CID
Integrafika Design Studio
1316 Folsom St.
San Francisco, CA 94103
phone 415-552-6876
fax 415-552-6877
integraf@msn.com
integraf@sirius.com
www.integrafika.com
(7)

MANUFACTURERS

Alchemy Glass & Light
3143 S. La Cienega Blvd.
Los Angeles, CA 90016
phone 310-836-8631
fax 310-836-8695
info@alchemyglass.com
www.alchemyglass.com
(81)

Artistic Tile
79 Fifth Ave.
New York, NY 10003
phone 212-727-9331;
    800-260-8486
fax 212-924-8481
moreinfo@artistictile.com
www.artistictile.com
(60)

Brass Light Gallery
P.O. Box 674
Milwaukee, WI 53201
phone 800-243-9595
fax 800-505-9404
customerservice@
    brasslight.com
www.brasslight.com
(22, 34, 35, 70, 73)

Brewster Wallcovering Co.
67 Pacella Park Dr.
Randolph, MA 02368
phone 781-963-4800; 800-
    366-1700
fax 781-963-4885
pbe@breup.com
www.brewsterwall
    covering.com
(53)

Craft-Maid Kitchens
501 S. Ninth St.
Bldg. C
Reading, PA 19602
phone 610-376-8686
fax 610-376-6998
craftmaid@talon.net
www.craft-maid.com
(126–127)

DACOR
phone 626-799-1000
www.dacor.com
(76)

Dura Supreme
300 Dura Dr.
Howard Lake, MN 55349
phone 888-711-3872
fax 800-242-3872
(120, 128–129)

Charlie Hallam
P.O. Box 5218
Crestline, CA 92325
phone 909-338-6174
fax 909-338-6134
Ebenzer@aol.com
(84, 92–93, 96–97)

Heritage Custom Kitchens
215 Diller Ave.
New Holland, PA 17578
phone 717-354-4011
fax 717-354-4487
www.hck.com
(144–145, 160–161)

Kichler Lighting
7711 E. Pleasant Valley Rd.
Cleveland, OH 44131-8010
phone 216-573-1000
fax 216-573-1001
dancer@kichler.com
www.kichler.com
(30)

Kohler Co.
444 Highland Dr.
Kohler, WI 53044-1515
phone 800-4-KOHLER
(11, 77, 232, 240–241,
    244–245, 246–247)

Neff Cabinets
6 Melanie Drive
Brampton, Ontario L6T 4K9
CANADA
phone 800-944-3833
fax 905-791-7788
(120, 136–137)

New West
2811 Big Horn Ave.
Cody, WY 82414
phone 800-653-2391
fax 327-527-7409
jmike@newwest.com
www.newwest.com
(45)

Priemia Cabinets
26929 Fraser Hwy.
Aldergrove, British Columbia
    V4W 3E4
CANADA
cabinets@tellus.net
(138–139)

Putnam Rolling Ladder Com-
    pany, Inc.
32 Howard St.
New York, NY 10013
phone 212-226-5147
fax 212-941-1836
putnam1905@aol.com
www.putnamrollingladder.com
(79)

Strittmatter Private Label
445 Main St.
Ridgefield, CT 06877
phone 203-438-7119
jstritt@aol.com
(154–155)

Style Craft Corp.
P.O. Box 458
Blue Ball, PA 17506
phone 717-445-6270
fax 717-445-5799
www.stylecraftcabinets.com
(28)

3M Mounting Products with Command Adhesive
c/o Montage
2982 Cleveland Ave. N.
Roseville, MN 55113
phone 800-577-8778 ext. 70
www.commandadhesive.com
(24)

Thomasville Furniture
401 E. Main St.
Thomasville, NC 27361
phone 800-225-0265
www.thomasville.com
(5, 199, 206–207, 226–227,
270–271, 272–273)

Velux America, Inc.
450 Old Brickyard Rd.
P.O. Box 5001
Greenwood, SC 29648-5001
phone 800-888-3589
fax 864-943-2631
www.velux-america.com
(302–303)

Wellborn Cabinet, Inc.
P.O. Box 1210
Ashland, AL 36251
phone 800-336-8040
fax 256-354-1874
mrooney@wellborn.com
www.wellborn.com
(28, 74)

York Wallcoverings
750 Linden Ave.
York, PA 17405
phone 717-846-4456
ad@yorkwall.com
www.yorkwall.com
(27)

PHOTOGRAPHERS

Abode Interiors UK
Albion Ct.
One Pierce St.
Macclesfield, Cheshire
   SK11 6ER
ENGLAND
phone 011-44-1625-500-070
fax 011-44-1625-500-910
(23, 50, 64, 65, 80, 124–125,
198, 202–203, 230, 231,
234–235, 236–237,
258–259, 262, 266–267)

Gordon Beall
5007 Elsmere Pl.
Bethesda, MD 20814
phone 301-581-0486
fax 301-581-0487
(10)

Beateworks
   **(Brad Simmons or Tim
   Street–Porter)**
2400 S. Shenandoah St.
Los Angeles, CA 90034
phone 310-558-1100
fax 310-842-8889
www.beateworks.com
(25, 132–133, 172, 182–183,
184–185, 212–213)

Beth Singer Photography
25741 River Dr.
Franklin, MI 48025
phone 248-626-4860
fax 248-932-3496
bsinger2@mindspring.com
(126–127)

Dan Bibb
155 Ridge St.
#6J
New York, NY 10002
phone 212-228-0103
(52)

Michael Blevins
105 W. Main St.
Ste. C
Bozeman, MT 59715
phone 406-582-5859
fax 406-582-4455
wedoadvertising@earthlink.net
(138–139)

Tom Bonner
1201 Abbot Kinney Blvd.
Venice, CA 90291
phone 310-396-7125
fax 310-396-4792
tsbphoto@aol.com
(67)

Brad Simmons Photography
870 Craintown Rd.
Perryville, KY 40468
phone 859-332-8400
fax 859-332-4433
www.bradsimmons.com
(40, 57, 59, 152–153)

Jim Brady
1010 University Ave.
#823
San Diego, CA 92103
phone 619-296-5304
fax 619-296-5304
(288–289)

Brian Vanden Brink
39 Curtis Ave.
Camden, ME 04843
phone 207-236-4035
fax 207-236-0704
(19, 55, 66, 110–111, 123,
168–169, 188–189,
190–191, 199, 214–215,
257, 274, 276, 283,
306–307, 308)

Mert Carpenter
Mert Carpenter Photography
202 Granada Way
Los Gatos, CA 95030
phone 408-370-1663
fax 408-370-1668
mert45fot6o@earthlink.net
(72)

Jim Cross
phone 510-459-0017
(250–251)

Edoardo D'Antona
Viale Del Lido 75
Rome 00122
ITALY
phone 011-39-06-560-0226
fax 011-39-06-560-0226
e.dantona@tin.it
(46, 62, 78, 130–131, 162–163)

Dennis Degnan
151 North Brook Rd.
West Chester, PA 19382
phone 610-793-2400
fax 610-793-2401
(264–265)

Kurt Dolnier
Greenwich, CT
phone 203-869-1932
(224–225)

Timothy Dunford
665 N. Beau Chere
No. 31
Mandeville, LA 70471
phone 504-845-4000
fax 504-845-4000
timbobby@earthlink.net
(84, 92–93, 96–97)

Phillip H. Ennis Photography
114 Millertown Rd.
Bedford, NY 10506
phone 914-234-9574
(contents, 8, 29, 41, 51, 63, 87,
88–89, 104–105, 108–109,
116–117, 118–119, 158–159,
164–165, 166–167, 197,
204–205, 216–217,
278–279, 296–297,
298–299, 300–301, back
cover)

Martin Fine
9842 Canby Ave.
Northridge, CA 91325
phone 818-341-7113
fax 818-341-7113
mfine@socal.rr.com
www.martfine.com
(150–151, 283, 292–293)

Curt Fischer
51 Stillman St.
San Francisco, CA 94107
(17, 242–243)

Nadine Frogger
3982 Camino de la Cumbre
Sherman Oaks, CA 91423
phone 818-386-1103
(194–195)

James Gabbard
8506 Holloway Dr.
West Hollywood, CA 90069
phone 310-659-9268
(134–135)

Jeff Hoatley
16 Cruise St.
Riverhead, NY 11901
phone 631-287-0366
(160–161)

The Interior Archive Ltd.
401 Fulham Rd.
London SW6 1EB
ENGLAND
phone 011-44-1713-700-595
fax 011-44-1819-602-695
www.interiorarchive.com
(48, 61, 180–181, 231,
248–249, 282, 286–287,
back cover)

John Sutton Photography
8 Main St.
Point San Quentin, CA 94964
phone 415-258-8100
fax 415-258-8167
john@johnsutton
photography.com
www.johnsuttonphoto
graphy.com
(49, 228–229)

Karen Ollis Photography
1547 Superior Ave.
Cleveland, OH 44114
phone 216-781-8646
fax 216-781-3040
ollistoula@earthlink.net
www.zdepth.com/ollis
(30)

Kaskel Architectual Photography, Inc.
5040 Warren
#407
Skokie, IL 60077
phone 847-675-8687
fax 847-675-8691
(28, 144–145)

Stefan Kirkeby
Pier 70
The Noonan Building 11
#106
San Francisco, CA 94107
phone 415-863-1950
fax 415-861-3864
skirk60588@aol.com
www.kirkebyphotography.com
(51)

Fred Knight
8 Via Brisa
Santa Fe, NM 87507
phone 505-424-1951
(120, 128–129, 136–137,
142–143)

Chris Lark
22720 Woodward Ave.
Ste. 202
Ferndale, MI 48220
phone 248-548-0280
fax 248-548-2868
(252–253, 285, 310–311)

David Duncan Livingston
1036 Erica Rd.
Mill Valley, CA 94941
phone 415-305-6050
fax 415-383-0897
ddl@davidduncanliving
ston.com
www.davidduncanliving
ston.com
(6, 21)

Peter Margonelli
20 Des Brosses St.
New York, NY 10014
phone 212-941-0380
(36)

Mark Lohman Photography
1021 S. Fairfax Ave.
Los Angeles, CA 90019
phone 323-933-3359
fax 310-471-6268
(contents, 66, 79, 83, 85, 86,
98–99, 100–101, 106–107,
122, 123, 146–147,
156–157, 178–179,
208–209, 238–239)

Mark Thomas Studio, Inc.
450 W. 31st St.
Ste. 9A
New York, NY 10001
phone 212-216-9205
fax 212-290-1105
mwthomas@bestweb.net
(232, 260–261)

John F. Martin
122 Paul Dr.
San Rafael, CA 94903
phone 415-472-4482
fax 415-472-4483
john@jfmdigital.com
www.jfmdigital.com
(7)

Robert Melnychuk
21587 W. 8th Ave.
Ste. 401
Vancouver, BC V6J 1T5
CANADA
phone 604-736-8066
(218–219, 233, 254–255)

Melabee M. Miller Photography
29 Beechwood Pl.
Hillside, NJ 07205
phone 908-527-9121
fax 908-527-0242
(68, 86, 102–103, 309)

Michael Morian
371 Broadway
2nd Fl.
New York, NY 10013
phone 212-334-4543
fax 212-226-2596
(47)

Phillip Nilsson
825 Ute Pass Rd.
Durango, CO 81301
phone 800-252-1027
(71)

Michael Partenio
14 Crosby St.
Danbury, CT 06810
phone 203-733-5598
(154–155, 268–269)

Marisa Pellegrini
Woodlawn, NJ
phone 212-679-7575
(172, 174–175)

Lawny Provo
100 N.E. 101 St.
Miami Shores, FL 33138
phone 305-608-5569
fax 305-608-5569
(18, 210–211)

Miki Rakicevic
1110 Camarillo St.
#124
West Toluca Lake, CA 91602
phone 818-505-1597
(222–223)

Eric Roth
P.O. Box 422
Topsfield, MA 01983
phone 978-887-1975
fax 978-887-5035
(196, 200–201, back cover)

Ron Ruscio
1090 Cherokee St.
#304
Denver, CO
phone 303-685-4796
(38)

Samu Studios
P.O. Box 165
Bay Port, NY 11705
phone 212-754-0415
www.samustudios.com
(contents, 75, 121, 122,
140–141, 148–149,
170–171, 233, 256, 275)

Tim Street-Porter
2704 Watsonia Terrace
Los Angeles, CA 90068
phone 323-874-4278
(cover, 9, 14, 15, 20, 26, 29, 39,
43, 44, 49, 54, 87, 90–91,
112–113, 114–115, 186–187,
263, 277)

Shaun Sullivan
Double Take Studio
614 Alabama St.
San Francisco, CA 94110
phone 415-648-5500
(12)

William Lesch Photography
426 S. Otero Ave.
Tucson, AZ 85701
phone 520-622-6693
fax 520-622-0701
wlesch@earthlink.net
(32, 54, 176–177)

OTHER

Ballard Designs
1670 Defoor Ave.
Atlanta, GA 30318
phone 800-367-2775
www.ballarddesigns.com
(263, 280–281)

Robert F. Mattice
1232 Vilanda
W. Covina, CA 91790
phone 626-917-8824
fax 626-917-8824
sixpenny2@aol.com
(71)

Joetta Moulden
9337-B Katy Freeway
#176
Houston, TX 77024
(57)

Seabrook Wallcoverings
1325 Farmville Rd.
Memphis, TN 38122
phone 901-320-3500
fax 901-320-3695
*www.seabrookwall
coverings.com*
(58, 284, 294–295)

Mark Wray
Mill Creek Post & Beam
P.O. Box 850
Saluda, NC 28773
phone 704-749-8000
(152–153)

Front cover: **Suzanne Rheinstein/Tim Street-Porter Photography**
Back cover: **Kuche Cucina/Amir Ilin/Phillip H. Ennis Photography** (left); **Simon McBride/The Interior Archive, Ltd.** (top);
Eric Roth/Janet Brown Interiors (right).
Abode Interiors UK: 23, 50, 64, 65, 80, 124, 125, 198, 202, 203, 230, 231 (top), 234, 235, 236, 237, 258, 259, 262, 266, 267;
Alchemy Glass & Light: 81; **Artistic Tile, Inc./William P. Steele Photography:** 60; **Ballard Designs:** 263 (bottom), 280, 281;
Beateworks.com: Brad Simmons: 132, 133, 172 (bottom), 184, 185, 212, 213; Tim Street-Porter: 182, 183; **Becker Interiors**
Inc./Omar Salinas Photography: 10; **Botkin Design/Dennis Degnan Photography:** 264, 265; **Brad Simmons Photography:**
40, 57, 59; Mark Wray: 152, 153; **Brass Light Gallery:** 22, 34, 35, 70, 73; **Brewster Wallcovering Co.:** 53; **Bytner Design**
Associates/Beth Singer Photography: 126, 127; **Carol R. Knott Interior Design:** 197 (bottom), 220, 221; **Lori W.**
Carroll/William Lesch Photography: 32, 54 (top), 176, 177; **Comprehensive Design/Curt Fischer Photography:** 17, 242, 243;
Custom Kitchens, Inc./Kaskel Architectual Photography, Inc.: 28 (top), 144, 145; **CW Design Company/Stefan Kirkeby**
Photography: 51 (bottom); **DACOR:** 76; **Darla's Unique & Chic Interiors/Miki Rakicevic Photography:** 222, 223; **David**
Duncan Livingston Photography: 21; **David M. Plante Interior Design/Peter Margonelli Photography:** 36; **Dennis Jenkins &**
Associates/Lawny Provo Photography: 18, 210, 211; **Double Take Studio/Shaun Sullivan Photography:** 12; **Eric Mitchell**
Shore Design/Timothy Dunford Photography: 84 (bottom), 92, 93, 96, 97; **Green & Co., Inc.:** Kurt Dolnier Photography: 224,
225; Marissa Pelligrini Photography: 172 (top), 174, 175; Phillip H. Ennis Photography: 63; **Greene & Proppe Design,**
Inc./Christopher Lark Photography: 252, 253, 285, 310, 311; **Gridley Company/Mert Carpenter Photography:** 72; **Joseph P.**
Horan: David Duncan Livingston Photography: 6; John Vaughan Photography: 69, 173, 192, 193, 304, 305; **Idea Company:**
Jeff Hoatley Photography: 160, 161; Michael Partenio Photography: 154, 155, 268, 269; **In-Site Design Group/R. Greg**
Hursley, Inc.: 85 (top), 94, 95, 290, 291; **Integrafika Design Studio/John F. Martin:** 7; **The Interior Archive, Ltd.:** Tim Bed-
dow: 287; Simon McBride: 231 (bottom), 248, 249; Christopher Simon Sykes: 180, 181; Fritz von der Schulenburg: 282, 286;
Andrew Wood: 48, 61; **Jane Bade Interiors/Martin Fine Photography:** 283 (top), 292, 293; **Janet Brown Interiors/Eric Roth**
Photography: 196, 200, 201; **Judy Campbell Interior Design, Inc./Phillip Nilsson Photography:** 71; **Kari Whitman Interi-**
ors/Nadine Foger Photography: 194, 195; **Kicher Lighting/Latina Homes/Karen Ollis Photography:** 30; **Kitchen Dimen-**
sions/Fred Knight Photography: 120, 128, 129, 136, 137, 142, 143; **Kohler Co.:** 11, 77, 232 (top), 240, 241, 244, 245, 246,
247; **Lifestyle Interior Design/Ron Ruscio Photography:** 38; **Mark Lohman Photography:** Contents (top), 66 (top), 79 (top),
83, 85 (bottom), 86 (top), 98, 99, 100, 101, 106, 107, 122, 146, 147, 156, 157, 178, 179, 208, 209, 238, 239; **Melabee M.**
Miller Photography: 68, 309; Adrienne Rich/A & R Interiors: 86 (bottom), 102, 103; **Mojo Stumer Associates/Phillip H. Ennis**
Photography: 8, 51 (top), 84 (top), 88, 89; **New West/Elijah Cobb Photography:** 45; **Phillip H. Ennis Photography:** 87 (top),
104, 105, 123 (bottom), 158, 159; Andrew Chary & Associates: 296, 297, 300, 301; Anne Cooper Interiors, Inc.: 41; Christo-
pher Coleman: 108, 109; Kuche Cucina/Amir Ilin: 164, 165; Darryl Wilson Design: 29 (bottom); Decor of Greenwich, Inc.: 278,
279; Green & Co., Inc.: 204, 205; Michael Whaley Interiors, Inc.: Contents (bottom), 197 (top), 216, 217; Mark Polo: 116, 117;
Trisha Reger: 298, 299; Lauren Rosenberg-Moffit: 166, 167; Samuel Botero Associates, Inc.: 87 (bottom), 118, 119; **Putman**
Rolling Ladder Co., Inc.: 79 (bottom); **Razvi Design Studio/Brady Architectural Photography:** 288, 289; **Robert Melnychuk**
Photography: 218, 219, 233 (top), 254, 255; **Ruder Finn, Inc./Thomasville Furniture:** 5, 199 (bottom), 206, 207, 226, 227,
270, 271, 272, 273; **Samu Studios:** Contents (center), 75, 121, 122, 140, 141, 148, 149, 170, 171, 275; Courtesy Hearst
Magazines: 233 (bottom), 256; **Sidnam Petrone Gartner Architects:** Michael Moran Photography: 47; Tim Street-Porter
Photography: 90, 91; **SieMatic Corporation/Mark Thomas Studio, Inc.:** 232 (bottom), 260, 261; **Square One Interiors/Jim**
Cross Photography: 250, 251; **Stacey Lapuk Interior Design, Inc./John Sutton Photography:** 49 (top), 228, 229; **Success N**
Marketing, Inc./Michael Blevins Photography: 138, 139; **Angelo Luigi Tartaglia/Edoardo D'Antona Photography:** 46, 62,
78, 130, 131, 162, 163; **Taylor & Company:** Dan Bibb Photography: 52; Tom Bonner Photography: 67; James Gabbard Photography: 134, 135; Pasadena Showcase House: 150, 151; **Thompson & Company/Seabrook Wallcoverings, Inc.:** Sandpiper
Studios "Antique Chic": 58; Seabrook Designs "Above & Beyond": 295; Seabrook Designs "Cuttin' Up": 284, 294; **3M Corpora-**
tion: 24; **Tim Street-Porter Photography:** 9, 14, 15, 20, 25, 26, 29 (top), 39, 43, 44, 49 (bottom), 54 (bottom), 87 (center),
112, 113, 114, 115, 186, 187, 263 (top), 277; **Brian Vanden Brink:** 19, 55, 66 (bottom), 123 (top), 168, 169, 199 (top), 214,
215, 283 (bottom), 306, 307; Burt & Weinrich Architects: 110, 111; Centerbrook Architects: 276; Drysdale Associates Interior
Design: 188, 189; Elliot & Elliot Architects: 308; John Gillespie: 274; Dominic Mercadante: 257; Susan Thorn Interior Design:
190, 191; **Velux America Inc.:** 302, 303; **Wellborn Cabinet, Inc.:** 28 (bottom), 74; **York Wallcoverings:** 27.